concrete
a studio design guide

michael stacey

The **Concrete** Centre

RIBA Publishing

contents

acknowledgements

Concrete: A Studio Design Guide is based on research conducted with the assistance of Anna Holden, John Inglis and Neil Evensen, who worked for the Manufacturing Architecture Research Centre, whilst undertaking their Professional Diploma in Architecture (RIBA Part 2) at London Metropolitan University. Martin Spencer, a RIBA Part 3 student at the University of Nottingham, has taken photographs especially for this book and worked on many of the illustrations with input from Robert Atkinson, a Diploma in Architecture (RIBA Part 2) student at the University of Nottingham. Professor Michael Stacey is Chair of Architecture at the University of Nottingham and director of Michael Stacey Architects.

The author wishes to thank Allan Haines, formerly of the Concrete Centre, for his support and guidance, Guy Thompson of the Concrete Centre and Adrian Ashby of Civil and Marine, Michael Currier of Schöck Ltd and Paul Scott of Adams Kara Taylor, and other contributors from the Concrete Centre for their input. Thanks also to Graham Farmer for co-organising field trips to visit the architecture of Fehn, Lewerentz and Utzon, to Darren Deane for his advice on Corbusier and Kahn, to Frances Stacey for her advice on clarity, and to James Thompson and Alex Lazarou for their editorial and graphical inputs.

FRONTISPIECE
Formwork of a slab of the German Industrial Tribunal in Erfurt
Architect: Gesine Weinmiller

Published by RIBA Publishing, 15 Bonhill Street, London EC2P 2EA

ISBN 978 1 85946 334 5

Stock code 69039

British Library Cataloguing in Publications Data
A catalogue record for this book is available from the British Library.

Publisher: Steven Cross
Commissioning Editor: James Thompson
Project Editor: Alex Lazarou
Designed and typeset by Alex Lazarou
Printed and bound by Polestar Wheatons

RIBA Publishing is part of RIBA Enterprises Ltd.
www.ribaenterprises.com

foreword

Concrete is a wonderful and versatile material. The elegance of concrete lies in its ability to provide enclosure, structure, and interior and exterior surface finishes, fire protection, thermal mass, and acoustic separation in a single construction material with no additional layers or treatments being required. It is this directness, combined with its tectonic and expressive qualities, that has appealed to architects from Frank Lloyd Wright to Le Corbusier, Louis Kahn, Tadao Ando, David Chipperfield, Sverre Fehn, Zaha Hadid, Herzog and de Meuron, Sanaa, Carlo Scarpa, Jørn Utson and Peter Zumthor – all featured in the pages of this guide. It explores how the latest constructional technology can be used to create the immutable qualities of architecture. Many of the projects possess a permanence that is shared with ancient architecture, which assisted in binding society together through symbolism, function and even poetry. Building to last and building in durability continue to be powerful principles for sustainable architecture.

The author, Professor Michael Stacey, has combined his experience and background in practice, research, teaching and writing to collect and explain the design potential of concrete. The end result is a book that deftly combines the visual and the inspirational with the level of detail more usually found in construction and engineering texts. It is a guide to concrete and how, when used intelligently, it can create excellent architecture. It includes photographs and drawings commissioned exclusively for this book. The Concrete Centre is delighted to support the research on which this guide is founded. It is an ideal book for both the student and practitioner alike, highlighting the full potential of the material and showing how concrete can address the key issues of today, including: climate adaptation, energy efficiency and material efficiency, and humankind's social and cultural needs. Concrete is primarily a national product using local materials and supporting local economies. The concrete industry has made huge steps to both develop and coordinate its sustainability and relevance to twenty-first-century architecture. This book provides architects, at all stages of their career, the information and inspiration to develop designs that are relevant to, and appropriate for, this century and beyond.

This guide has been written to be accessible, yet it can be used to inform a project specification – keep a copy in your design studio next to your laptop or drawing board, whether this is in your school of architecture or in practice.

Guy CW Thompson RIBA
HEAD OF ARCHITECTURE & SUSTAINABILITY
THE CONCRETE CENTRE

www.concretecentre.com

1.1 Phaeno Science Centre, Wolfsburg, Germany
Designed by Zaha Hadid Architects; Engineer: Adams Kara Taylor

ONE **plasticity**

'I like architecture to have some raw, vital, earthy quality. You do not
have to make concrete perfectly smooth or paint it or polish it. If you
consider changes in the play of light on a building before it's built,
you can vary the colour and feel of concrete by daylight alone.'
Zaha Hadid [1]

The beauty of concrete is its plasticity. It will take on the form of its mould with effectively no geometric limitations, except possibly in edge details. Concrete takes on the texture of the mould surface, be it the smoothness of a steel shutter or the texture of a timber board. It is readily produced on site as in situ concrete, or offsite as precast concrete, with all the benefits of factory-based manufacturing. The origin of the versatility of concrete is its plasticity – some call it liquid stone. Examples of high-quality precast concrete truly mimic stone, deserving the term used by the concrete industry, artificial stone.

These precast units have the fine quality and detail achieved by the subtracted craft of a mason. Concrete may be used to make one-off projects, such as the highly expressive TWA Terminal by Eero Saarinen in New York, or standardised products, such as precast concrete floor planks. Exploration of the potential of digital design to liberate the realisation of architecture has led to an increased interest in formable materials, which is eloquently demonstrated by the Phaeno Science Centre, in Wolfsburg, Germany, by Zaha Hadid Architects and engineers Adams Kara Taylor.

1.2 TWA Terminal in New York,
which opened in 1962
Architect: Eero Saarinen

1.3 Detail of the curvilinear concrete
of the TWA Terminal, New York

1.4   Contemporary photograph of the Penguin Pool
at Regent's Park Zoo
Designed by: Berthold Lubetkin of Tecton; Engineer: Ove Arup

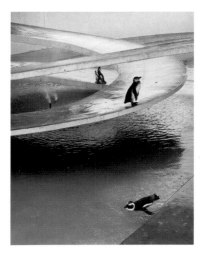

1.5   The finely dimensioned concrete ramps of
the Penguin Pool at Regent's Park Zoo, London,
photographed when it opened in 1934

This chapter sets out the potential of concrete in the creation of high-quality contemporary architecture, using exemplars from the twentieth and twenty-first century. The following chapters explore key technical opportunities and constraints. The book ends with a discussion of how to produce concrete on a sustainable basis and its vital role in the generation of a sustainable built environment.

1.6   Tadao Ando's characteristic smooth in situ concrete with
expressed and carefully regulated shutter bolt recesses
in the Koshino House, Ashiya, Japan

The shape of concrete is entirely dependent on its mould or formwork. During the construction of in situ concrete, a fascinating precursor, or virtual architecture, is created by the formwork and its structural supports. The space of the building is often occupied by the formwork, while voids define where the concrete structure is to be (Figure 1.14). Tadao Ando became interested in concrete as it offered him the potential to create a new architecture for Japan, inspired by twentieth-century modernist architects such as Le Corbusier. Yet, the timber formwork offered an opportunity to continue the timber craft tradition, as demonstrated in Japanese Buddhist temples. Ando noted, at a conference on concrete and architecture in London during 1992, that the carpenters making shuttering for his projects in Japan would expect to achieve a tolerance of ±1 mm in 6,000 mm. The precision of his concrete is a result of cultural continuity and the continuity of this craft tradition. The exemplary use of concrete by Swiss architects, as exemplified by Peter Märkli, is facilitated by a continuity of carpentry craft traditions within Switzerland.

1.7   The daylight interior of La Congiunta
Architect: Peter Märkli

1.8   The Chapel in Olavsundet, Ny-Hellesund
Designed by: Sverre Fehn

1.9   The interior of the Chapel in Olavsundet, Ny-Hellesund

The Chapel in Olavsundet, Ny-Hellesund, designed by Sverre Fehn in 1999, is a raw example of concrete's elemental power, it remains of the earth. Sverre Fehn intended: 'The structure puts the landscape on the stage, and the light and the openings become fragments of the horizon.' The interior of the Chapel with its four wooden doors and concave concrete wall is 'like being in a room that demonstrates time'.[2]

The curvilinear geometry of the roof of Le Corbusier's Chapel of Nôtre Dame du Haut, at Ronchamp, is generated by straight lines, which form a ruled geometry (Figure 1.16). This greatly facilitated the fabrication of the formwork as it was made of timber boards. It is vital that the formwork is stiff enough to resist the bursting pressure of the wet concrete and that it is well sealed to avoid the loss of liquid.

Concrete can also be finished after the formwork is removed (or struck). This ranges from grit blasting to all of the techniques used by masons on stone, which are explored in Chapter 4.

The advantages of using concrete are its:

- formability;
- robustness and durability;
- strength;
- inherent resistance to fire;
- acoustic damping qualities;
- thermal mass; and
- diversity of finishes and texture.

1.10 Sydney Opera House
      Architect: Jørn Utzon;
      Structural engineer: Ove Arup

1.12 A ground beam under construction in Granada:
      –   placing the primary rebar (top)
      –   tying the rebar cages together (middle)
      –   shuttered ready for the concrete
          to be poured (bottom)

1.11 The Cangarde equestrian sculpture,
      Castlevecchio, Verona
      Architect: Carlo Scarpa

Concrete can deliver these performative qualities cost-effectively when appropriately used in contemporary construction. Concrete is a radical material, however, it can bridge between eras – it can appear very modern in the hands of Eero Saarinen, Jørn Utzon or Zaha Hadid, or it can evoke its origins in ancient Rome, some two thousand years ago.[3] Carlo Scarpa in the restoration of Castlevecchio, Verona (1958 to 1964), uses a carefully considered palette of materials, including concrete, copper and bronze for the new elements.[4] Concrete is used in a bold manner in the restoration. In particular, in the cantilevered in situ concrete support of the stone Cangarde equestrian sculpture that dates from circa 1335.

1.13 *House* (from 1993; since demolished)
Artist: Rachel Whiteread

Rachel Whiteread's *House* from 1993, which was commissioned and produced by Art Angel, eloquently demonstrates the capacity of cast concrete to acquire the detail of the 'formwork'. Whiteread used an existing terraced house in the East End of London to cast this sculpture.

Concrete is strong in compression and weak in tension. Only elements such as foundations are formed of concrete alone: this is known as mass concrete, and foundations may need reinforcement depending on the ground conditions. To create elements that act under tension and compression, it is necessary to add reinforcement. This predominantly comprises high-tensile steel, however, in areas where there is a significant risk of corrosion, stainless steel should be used.

1.14 Formwork of the reinforced in situ concrete of a structural cone during the construction of the Phaeno Science Centre

One alternative to stainless steel reinforcement is polymer composite reinforcement, which has the advantage of being lighter. Steel, synthetic or glass fibres, dispersed throughout the concrete, may be used as a substitute for reinforcement to provide tensile strength to the concrete, see Chapter 8 on thinness and form. In the structural cones of the Phaeno Science Centre, the proportion of the reinforced concrete that comprises steel reinforcement is only approximately 6%, when measured by weight. A more typical proportion for reinforcement is between 2 and 5%. The cones of the Phaeno Science Centre have a very significant structural and spatial role in the project.

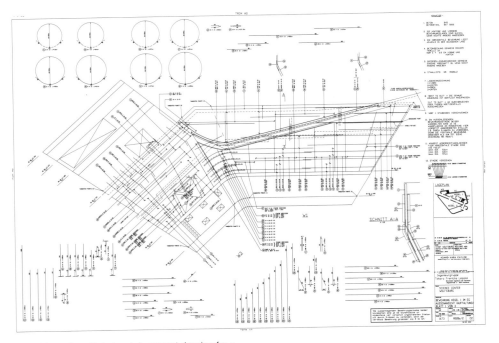

1.15 Adams Kara Taylor's reinforcement drawing for a structural cone of the Phaeno Science Centre

Well-specified and carefully constructed
reinforced concrete has an inherent life
expectancy of over one hundred years – it is
a very durable material from which to create
architecture. While designing the Chapel of
Nôtre Dame du Haut, Ronchamp, Le Corbusier
stated: 'Here we will build a monument
dedicated to nature and we will make it our
lives' purpose.'[5]

1.16 Chapel of Nôtre Dame du Haut, Ronchamp,
photographed after its opening in 1955
Architect: Le Corbusier

2.1 The galleries of Yale Art Gallery
Architect: Louis Kahn

'If you are dealing with concrete, you must know the order of the concrete. You must know its nature, what concrete strives to be. Concrete wants to be granite, but can't quite make it. The reinforcing rods in it are a play of secrets workers that make this so called molten stone appear marvelously capable.'
Louis Kahn[1]

Concrete is a technology that is over 4,000 years old. The Romans made concrete using crushed volcanic pozzolanic rocks, named after the tuffs at Pozzuoli near Naples. Pozzolanic rock has a chemical composition that reacts with calcium hydroxide at ambient temperature to form cementitious properties. The word concrete is based on the Latin *concretus*, which means 'bring together' and represents its composite – the bringing together of materials with diverse properties where the whole is greater than the sum of the component elements.

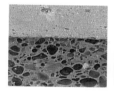

2.2   Cross section showing the matrix of concrete

Concrete is formed by mixing carefully controlled quantities of cement, sand, aggregate and water. Cement undergoes a chemical reaction when mixed with water, becoming hydrated by water and gradually hardening. On curing, the water that remains unbound to the calcium in the cement evaporates, leaving air gaps. Correctly balancing the water content of concrete is key to its strength. The percentage by weight of fully cured concrete, with a density of between 2,250 and 2,400 kg/m^3, is 6% water, 14% cement and 80% aggregate.

2.3   The primary materials or ingredients in a concrete mix – water, sand, aggregate, Portland cement and ggbs

Cement

The most commonly used cement in contemporary construction is Portland cement. It was patented in 1824 by Joseph Aspdin. Portland cement is manufactured by mixing finely ground limestone or chalk, clay and sand, and heating it almost to melting point (about 1,450°C) in a large rotating kiln. The cement clinker that emerges is then ground to a powder to which about 5% gypsum is added to control the setting time of the cement.

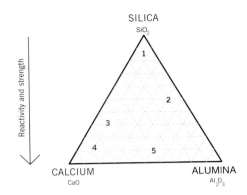

1 Glass
2 Fly ash
3 Ground granulated blastfurnace slag
4 Portland cement
5 Calcium aluminium cements

2.4   The basic chemistry of concrete

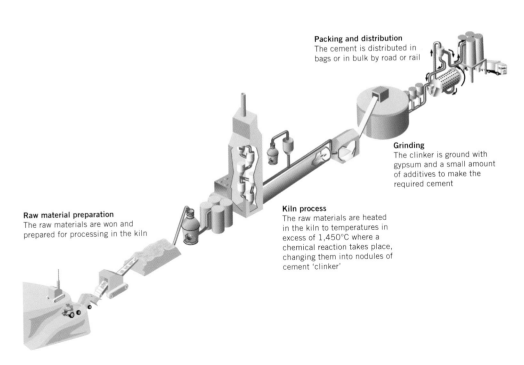

Packing and distribution
The cement is distributed in bags or in bulk by road or rail

Grinding
The clinker is ground with gypsum and a small amount of additives to make the required cement

Raw material preparation
The raw materials are won and prepared for processing in the kiln

Kiln process
The raw materials are heated in the kiln to temperatures in excess of 1,450°C where a chemical reaction takes place, changing them into nodules of cement 'clinker'

2.5   Diagram of the production of cement

Aggregate

Aggregates used in concrete range in size, however they are strictly graded. The range is from sand, which is defined as fine particles of 0.063 mm up to 2 mm, to small stones that typically range between 2 mm and 22 mm.[2] The requirements for concrete aggregates is given in BS EN 12620: 2002 *Aggregates for Concrete*, and guidance document PD 6682-1:2003 *Aggregates*. While the main purpose of aggregates in concrete is to restrain the shrinkage, which occurs in cement paste alone, they also act as a low-cost filler. Concrete produced without sand is called no-fines concrete and can be used to create water-permeable surfaces. This is of significance in reducing peak storm-water runoff from paved surfaces and can form part of a sustainable urban drainage strategy. A wide range of stone can be used as aggregate; they should be tested for their suitability and for the presence of any organic substances that may inhibit hardening or durability. The key properties of aggregates are: density, cleanliness, moisture content, grain form, surface texture and hardness. Aggregates are graded by using standardised sieves and the proportions are determined by weight.

Water

Typically, drinking water is used to make concrete. The water to cement ratio is critical to the production of a successful mix; cement will hydrate with a water–cement ratio of only 1 to 0.22, however a typical mix is 1 to 0.5 in order to achieve workability. Voids left by evaporating excess water reduce the strength of the concrete, while the increased porosity makes it susceptible to water ingress via capillary action and, thus, potentially to frost damage. The concrete will also have a greater risk of cracking from shrinkage. Hardened concrete forms a stable matrix for structural components, and it is vital that the number of voids formed by evaporation are minimised. If premature drying occurs, this will create a friable sandy surface to the concrete.

Admixture

Chemical admixtures are introduced into the mix to either improve the workability of the concrete or to improve its performance once cured. The primary types of admixture can make the following changes to the properties of the concrete by:

- improving the workability of the concrete, making it easier to place without reduction in strength;
- reducing the water content of the concrete and, hence, increasing its strength;
- accelerating or retarding the setting and strength gain of the concrete;
- entraining air bubbles to improve resistance to freeze thaw cycles – this is achieved by interrupting the capillaries created by the evaporated water and can decrease the thermal conductivity, providing a lower U-value; and
- reducing the shrinkage of the hardened concrete.

2.6   Nordic Pavilion for Biennale in Venice, 1962
Architect: Sverre Fehn

2.7   Detail of the 1,000 mm by 600 mm in situ concrete
beams that are at 523 mm centres that also act as
the brie soleil of the Nordic Pavilion

The colour of concrete

Without post-treatment, the colour of the concrete is defined by the smallest particles in the mix: cement and sand. To produce a white concrete, white cement is required: a Portland cement with low iron content, white sand and white aggregate. Glass produced from sand with a low iron content is very clear and is often described as water white glass. Ground pigments, with a particle size of about 50 microns, may be used to adjust the colour as they are even finer than sand (Chapter 4 looks in greater detail at the finishing and colour of concrete). In 1962, Sverre Fehn used white concrete for the structure of the Nordic Pavilion at the Biennale in Venice to create a shadowless northern light. He specified 'white cement, white sand and crushed white marble'.[3] He used an essentially similar specification for the white concrete of the Ivar Aasen Centre, which was completed in 2000. Sverre Fehn worked for a year with Jean Prouvé, the pioneer of lightweight folded metal-based architecture, and this influence can be read at times in the elemental nature of his planning. Sverre Fehn had an affinity with concrete, particularly board-marked concrete where traces of the timber shuttering remain.

Alternatives to cement

A range of materials are available to replace or combine with Portland cement in a concrete mix – in all cases the cement needs to act as a hydraulic binder. The primary cementatious materials that are an alternative to Portland cement are:

- pozzolanic rocks;
- ground granulated blastfurnace slag (ggbs);
- fly ash;
- silica fume;
- calcium-sulfoaluminate-based cements;
- geopolymeric cements;
- burnt shale;
- magnesium-oxide-based cements; and
- limestone flour (fine limestone dust).

The primary reason for using an alternative to Portland cement is to reduce the embodied energy and embodied CO_2 of the concrete. Embodied energy is the quantity of energy required to produce a material and must take into account all the processes, from extraction to manufacture, that contribute to the energy needed. The embodied CO_2 is the sum of all of the CO_2 required to produce a material, which may arise from the process or the energy required to drive it – related greenhouse gases produced also need to be considered. Data on embodied energy and embodied CO_2 for concrete are provided in Chapter 10. BS EN 197-1: 2000 *Cement* lists the 11 groups of factory-produced cements that are readily available in Europe, including blended cements incorporating ggbs and fly ash.

For further discussion on the manufacture of cement and for an introduction to BS EN 197-1: 2000 *Cement*, see *Architectural Insitu Concrete* by David Bennett.[4]

Table 2.1: Reproduction of Table 1 from BS EN 197-1: 2000 *Cement*
— the 27 products in the family of common cements

Main types	Notation of the 27 products (types of common cement)		Composition (percentage by mass*)		
			Main constituents		
			Clinker	Blast-furnace slag	Silica fume
			K	S	D†
CEM I	Portland cement	CEM I	95–100	–	–
CEM II	Portland-slag cement	CEM IV/A-S	80–94	6–20	–
		CEM IV/~B-S	65–79	21 to 35	–
	Portland-silica fume cement	CEM IV/A-D	90–94	–	6–10
	Portland-pozzolana cement	CEM II/A-P	80–94	–	–
		CEM II/B-P	65–79	–	–
		CEM II/A-Q	80–94	–	–
		CEM II/B-Q	65–79	–	–
	Portland-fly ash cement	CEM II/A-V	80–94	–	–
		CEM II/B-V	65–79	–	–
		CEM II/A-W	80–94	–	–
		CEM II/B-W	65–79	–	–
	Portland-burnt shale cement	CEM II/A-T	80–94	–	–
		CEM II/B-T	65–79	–	–
	Portland-limestone cement	CEM II/A-L	80–94	–	–
		CEM II/B-L	65–79	–	–
		CEM II/A-LL	80–94	–	–
		CEM II/B-LL	65–79	–	–
	Portland-composite cement‡	CEM II/A-M	80–94		
		CEM II/B-M	65–79		
CEM III	Blastfurnace cement	CEM III/A	35–64	36–65	–
		CEM III/B	20–34	66–80	–
		CEM III/C	5–19	81–95	–
CEM IV	Pozzolanic cement‡	CEM IV/A	65–89	–	
		CEM IV/B	45–64	–	
CEM V	Composite cement‡	CEM V/A	40–64	18–30	–
		CEM V/B	20–38	31–50	–

*   The values in the table refer to the sum of the main and minor additional constituents.
†   The proportion of silica fume is limited to 10%.
‡   In Portland-composite cements CEM II/A-M and CEM II/B-M, in Pozzolanic cements CEM IV/A and CEM IV/B and in Composite cements CEM V/A and CEM V/B the main constituents besides clinker shall be declared by designation of the cement.

Composition (percentage by mass*)							
Main constituents							Minor additional constituents
Pozzolana		Fly ash		Burnt shale	Limestone		
Natural	Natural calcine	Siliceous	Calcareous				
P	Q	V	W	T	L	LL	
–	–	–	–	–	–	–	0–5
–	–	–	–	–	–	–	0–5
–	–	–	–	–	–	–	0–5
–	–	–	–	–	–	–	0–5
6–20	–	–	–	–	–	–	0–5
21–35	–	–	–	–	–	–	0–5
–	6–20	–	–	–	–	–	0–5
–	21–35	–	–	–	–	–	0–5
–	–	6–20	–	–	–	–	0–5
–	–	21–35	–	–	–	–	0–5
–	–	–	6–20	–	–	–	0–5
–	–	–	21–35	–	–	–	0–5
–	–	–	–	6–20	–	–	0–5
–	–	–	–	21–35	–	–	0–5
–	–	–	–	–	–	–	0–5
–	–	–	–	–	21–35	–	0–5
–	–	–	–	–	–	6–20	0–5
–	–	–	–	–	–	21–35	0–5
6–20					–	–	0–5
21–35					–	–	0–5
–	–	–	–	–	–	–	0–5
–	–	–	–	–	–	–	0–5
–	–	–	–	–	–	–	0–5
11–35				–	–	–	0–5
36–55				–	–	–	0–5
18–30			–	–	–	–	0–5
31–50			–	–	–	–	0–5

2.8 A ready-mix lorry providing a reliable and local delivery of specific and batched concrete mixes

2.9 Ready-mixed concrete being pumped into place at the Jones House, Randalls Town, Northern Ireland
Designed by Allan Jones Architects

The development of ready-mixed concrete brought a greater degree of certainty to the production of high-quality concrete. It was first introduced in 1909, however, it did not become a significant mode of delivery in Britain until the 1960s. It now accounts for about three-quarters of concrete used for site-based construction. This is a locally-based industry; in the UK the average distance from a ready-mix plant to site is five miles, and half of all plants are located at an aggregate extraction site.[5]

Pozzolanic rocks and industrial by-products

Volcanic rocks, such as tuff of Italy, trass from the upper Rhine and santourin from Greece, have pozzolanic qualities when ground – they hydrate in the presence of water. Instead of a return to the use of naturally occurring pozzolans as an alternative to Portland cement, there is an increasing interest in the use of industrial by-products, which may be described as a form of industrial-ecology. Their use has the potential to significantly reduce the embodied energy of concrete, as well as the quantity of primary raw material that needs to be excavated and processed (see Chapter 10).

2.10 A vertical roller mill grinding ggbs at the Civil and Marine works in Purfleet

2.11 Ggbs was used in the concrete mix of the structure of the Empire State Building, completed 1931
Designed by William F. Lamb of Shreve, Lamb and Harmon

Ggbs
This alternative to Portland cement is a by-product of iron and steel manufacture. Molten slag is dragged from a blast-furnace, rapidly cooled with water, and then ground to a fine, glassy white powder. It is classified as a latent hydraulic material, which means it has pozzolanic cementitious properties. These properties are only activated when ggbs is combined with Portland cement to initiate the hydration process – ggbs can comprise up to about 70% of the cement mix. Ggbs is not a new product, and was used in the construction of the Empire State Building, completed in 1931.

2.12 Ggbs was used in the concrete of Canary Wharf Underground Station, London
Designed by Foster and Partners, completed 1999

Ggbs offers a number of advantages:

- improved durability, and resistance to the ingress of water is reduced as capillary paths left by the evaporating water are interrupted;
- a low risk of thermal cracking;
- resistance to sulphate attack;
- whiter colours; and
- reduced embodied energy.

It was specified for Canary Wharf Underground Station on the Jubilee Line by Foster and Partners in order to provide an economical whiter concrete, which was vital to achieve a good reflectance for the up lighting of the station concourse. One disadvantage of using ggbs to replace a high proportion of Portland cement is that the concrete takes longer to harden, particularly in cold temperatures. It also takes longer to reach its full strength when compared with a mix based wholly on Portland cement. For the conversion of a Victorian public library into the Creative Media Training Centre for the London Borough of Southwark, the architect Architype proposed to use a concrete mix with 72% ggbs and 28% Portland cement, with the aim of minimising the embodied energy in the new concrete elements. The contactor, however, could not manage the delay to the building programme resulting from the slower gain in strength, particularly in cold weather. Eventually a compromise was reached and a 50% ggbs concrete mix was used. For more information on ggbs, see BS EN 15167-1:2006 *Ggbs* and Chapter 10 where the benefits of using ggbs are further developed.

2.13 The piers of Falkirk Wheel under construction using a concrete mix that includes fly ash

2.14 The Falkirk Wheel canal boatlift, completed 2002
Designed by Ove Arup and Partners, Butterley Engineering and RMJM architects

Fly ash
Typically a fine grey powder – fly ash is a by-product of coal fire power stations and is electrostatically precipitated from the exhaust gases. It is defined as an artificial pozzolan and is typically used in combination with Portland cement. Its advantages are:

- improved cohesion;
- improved workability; and
- reduced embodied energy.

Fly ash can be used to manufacture cements in accordance with BS EN 197-1 *Cement* categories CEM II and CEM IV.

Silica fume
This very fine powder is highly pozzolanic and it can be difficult to handle. However, concrete produced with silica fume offers very high strength and good durability. It is a by-product of the manufacturing of silicon and metal alloys containing silicon in electric arc furnaces. Its advantages are:

- very high strength and good durability; and
- reduced embodied energy.

The specification and use of silica fume in concrete is defined by BS EN 13263: 2005.

Alternative cements
The concrete industry is actively researching alternative cements with a low environmental imprint, including:

- calcium-sulfoaluminate-based cements;
- geopolymeric cements; and
- magnesium-oxide-based cements.

Presently these are appropriate only for specialist applications or currently have low availability in the UK.

Ultra high-strength concrete
The properties of concrete may be modified to establish an ultra high-strength building material comparable to the properties of metals. Ultra high-strength concrete has been continually developed since the 1950s when 34 MPa (34 N/mm^2) was considered high-strength. A typical strength for a structural concrete today is 40 MPa. Currently, by using an ultra high-strength mix, it is possible to achieve a compressive strength of up to 200 MPa for in situ concrete. High-strength concrete columns can hold more weight and, therefore, can be made slimmer than regular strength concrete columns, thereby offering more useable space, particularly in the lower

2.15 The close-moulded concrete shells at Shawnessy Light Rail Station, Calgary, which are only 20 mm thick, are an exemplar of ultra high-strength concrete
Architect by Enzo Vicenzino

floors of buildings. Ultra high-strength concrete is also applicable to precast thin, lightweight structural elements, such as balcony slabs and slender staircases.

Types of high-strength concrete

Macro defect free
One of the first breakthroughs in the development of high-strength concrete technology was macro defect free (MDF) cement. It was developed in the 1970s by ICI Special Projects, by a team lead by Derel Birchall. The aim of MDF was to create a material to replace plastics and lightweight metals such as aluminium. MDF requires significantly less embodied energy to produce, as it does not need to be melted at relatively high temperatures to become formable, as concrete hardens at room temperature. Voids form in the cement paste due to air entrapment during mixing and from the pores formed within the material during hydration. Consequentially, cement paste, when set, has a lower tensile and bending strength than plastic and metal. The removal of these flaws in the

cement paste is the predominant factor in establishing a concrete of high-tensile strength. By introducing a small quantity of water-soluble polymers into the cement and water, particles in the mix become more closely packed, which significantly increases the tensile strength.

Techniques such as MDF consequently initiated the development of polymer paste. The paste is created by mixing the MDF until it is virtually dry and becomes a mouldable putty. This is rolled to eliminate air bubbles and is then formed using conventional plastic pressing operations. Incorporating fibres, such as glass, can further enhance the strength of MDF cement to exceed that of aluminium. Injection moulding or extruding MDF products allow the production of products such as door handles and furniture, which could only normally be formed with plastics or metals.

Dense Silica Particle
Conceived a few years later, Dense Silica Particle (DSP) cement is an alternative to MDF. It follows the same principle of minimising the void spaces between cement grains to achieve high strength. In DSP cement, this is enabled

2.16 Spiral staircase in the Tuborg 15 Building, Copenhagen, precasted using CRC
Designed by Arkitema Architects with
engineers Ramboll Consultants

through the addition of a fine silica additive with a particle size of 0.1 μm (1 x 10⁻⁶ mm). As a result, workability was achieved based on a chemical reaction between the silica and the cement paste, plus the addition of a small amount of water and a super-plasticiser. The limitation of DSP is that, without the addition of fibre reinforcement, it can have a low-tensile strength when compared with MDF. It does, however, compare favourably with MDF when subjected to compression forces.

Compact Reinforced Composite
Compact Reinforced Composite (CRC) concrete adopts and combines the qualities of both MDF and DSP concrete to establish a mix that is both workable and ultra high-strength. As with DSP, workability is achieved through the addition of a very fine silica additive. To achieve a higher tensile strength, steel fibre reinforcement is added to create a mix with a very high bond strength that provides robustness and ductility. CRC has a mortar-like consistency and contains only very fine aggregates that allow for very close rebar spacing, making it suitable for very thin structural elements. It can be used for both precast construction and in situ, as it is in the form of a dry mortar with binder, sand and steel fibres, with water being the only ingredient that needs adding. CRC has a typical mean compressive strength of 150 MPa. It can also be used as a welding tool to 'glue' together narrow joints between reinforced concrete sections.

The spiral staircase in the atrium of Tuborg 15 Building, Copenhagen, designed by Arkitema Architects with engineers Ramboll Consultants, was only realisable in precast concrete by the use of CRC. It was developed in 1986 by CRC Technology of Aalborg, Denmark. The spiral staircase was completed in 2002 and David Bennett, in *Concrete Quarterly*, described his surprise and delight on seeing it:

> 'Standing four floors tall, looking like a paper streamer hanging from the ceiling, is a pencil-thin, smooth, white, spiral staircase. It seems impossible that anything so slender, so elegant and so dramatically curved could possibly be cast in concrete. Surely it must be steel or aluminium? You take a closer look, you walk up the elegant fan-tailed flights, but you can still scarcely believe that this really is concrete.'[6]

The staircase was precast in CRC by Beton-Tegl and installed by NCC Denmark. It has an overall diameter of 6 m and the central structural spiral beam has a diameter of 1.5 m. The spiral beam is 1,500 mm high and 150 mm thick, and was cast in four sections. The stair treads are cast in 16 identical sections, comprising six treads. Each tread cantilevers 2,250 mm and tapers from 100 mm to 30 mm at the edge and contains 8 mm diameter reinforcing bars. CRC is mid-grey when cast and the staircase has been painted white, which also disguises the 'stitching together' of the precast sections.

Ductal®

This is another CRC concrete that is based on the principles of MDF and DSP, which is produced by co-owners Lafarge, Bouygues and Rhodia. As well as the incorporation of steel fibres and the elimination of voids through the addition of a silica additive, Ductal relies on pre-stressing to achieve the ultimate compressive strength (200–800 MPa) and load-carrying capacity. Pressure is applied to the concrete mix before and after setting, and then the finished product is subjected to 90°C heat treatment for up to three days. Although this creates a very high compressive strength concrete, it is inevitably an expensive procedure and may not always be appropriate for a project. Pre-stressing provides Ductal with considerable strength, which, in addition to its lightweight and thin nature, makes it suitable for building components that would only usually be possible in steel or aluminium.

The performance characteristics of Ductal–FM Grey: 2GM2.0 are as follows:

- Cure time at 20°C 24 hours after pour > 30 MPa.
- Cure time at 20°C 24 hours after pour > 150 MPa.
- Resistance to compression 150–180 MPa.
- Resistance to flex 30–40 MPa.
- Young's Modulus 50,000 MPa.
  (Data courtesy of Lafrage.)

Sherbrooke Footbridge

The first major structure to use Ductal (200 MPa) was a 60 m span truss footbridge in Sherbrooke, Quebec, Canada, in 1995. The walkway slab, which is only 30 mm thick and 3.3 m wide, acts as the stiffening top chord of the 3 m deep truss. The struts and tension ties that connect the top and bottom chord members are thin-walled stainless steel tubes filled with Ductal. Confining the concrete in external tubing enhances the compressive strength to 350 MPa. The bottom chord

2.17 Sherbrooke Footbridge, photographed in 2006

comprises twin Ductal beams that are 320 mm wide by 380 mm deep. External post-tensioning tendons, placed longitudinally, pass through the bottom chord beams, while the 30 mm top slab is transversely pre-stressed. No rebar was used for any part of the structure, not even for distribution steel. Sherbrooke Footbridge was built by Bolduc and Béton Canada Bouygues.

Seonyu Footbridge

A footbridge was built over the river Han in Seoul for the 2002 Football World Cup. Called Seonyu Footbridge, it is more commonly known as the 'Bridge of Peace' and was designed by architect Rudy Ricciotti. It has two approach spans constructed in steel and a central 120 m double arch, cast using Ductal. The tee-shaped structure of the arch is 1.3 m deep with a walkway 4.3 m wide, which is only 30 mm deep. This bridge demonstrates the visual elegance that can be achieved using ultra high-strength concrete.

2.18 Seonyu Footbridge, completed 2002
Architect: Rudy Ricciotti

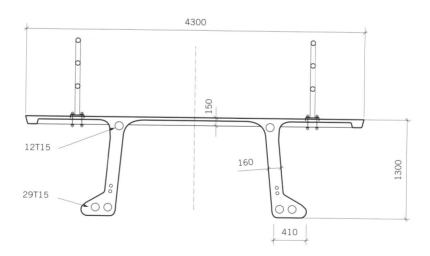

2.19 Seonyu Footbridge – section

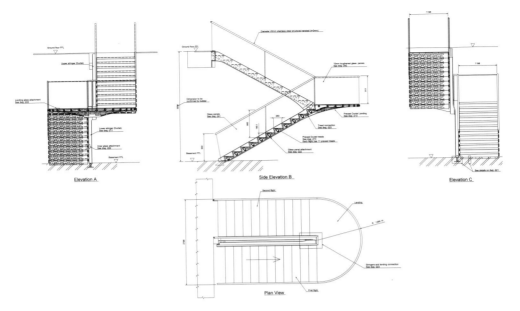

2.20 Drawing of the proposed new staircase at the Building Centre, London, which is to be formed from Ductal

Engineers: Price & Myers

Staircase in the Building Centre

The first application of Ductal in the UK was due to be a new staircase within the Building Centre, London, designed by engineers Price & Myers. The drawing promises a staircase that is both finely and richly detailed. Currently this project is on hold due to the banking-led recession of the end of the first decade of the twenty-first century and the resultant weak Pound. Ductal is produced in France and thus sold in Euros.

Self-compacting concrete

This is a relatively new product that is ideal for achieving enhanced finishes and compaction within complex geometries, where the reinforcement may be at close centres and vibration of the wet concrete would prove difficult. Self-compacting concrete is produced offsite by the addition of a superplasticiser and a stabiliser to the mix. The addition of these chemical additives significantly increases the ease and rate of flow, enabling faster construction times and ease of workability. Self-compacting concrete is suitable for both in situ and precast construction. The superplasticiser makes the mortar softer and more flexible, allowing it to flow into the moulds without the need for vibration compaction. Self-compacting concrete is being increasingly used by the precast industry as it minimises the health and safety risk related to mechanical vibration techniques, and reduces labour costs while improving the visual quality of the units by minimising surface air-bubbles.

The stabiliser is required to give the concrete mix more viscosity, so that, when it is poured around a reinforcement or obstacles, displacement of the aggregates is kept to a minimum, preventing the mortar and aggregate from separating. It also promotes compaction due to the increased weight of the mix, which allows every part of the mould to be filled by means of the concrete's self-weight. The additives enable the concrete to have a faster setting time. To prevent cold joints, it is therefore important to have a continuous supply of mixture. A cold joint is a joint between two sections of concrete where one side has set – sometimes known as day work joints – structural continuity is provided by the reinforcing bars, known as starter bars, see Figure 3.5. Further information on self-compacting concrete can be sourced from www.ermco.eu.

2.21 Self-compacting concrete – testing the concrete mix for the Phaeno Science Centre

Phaeno Science Centre

The Phaeno Science Centre in Wolfsburg, Northern Germany, was designed by Zaha Hadid Architects to achieve a seamless transition between the vertical and horizontal elements of the structural system. In response to this integrated geometry, the structure of this project was analysed by engineers Adams Kara Taylor as a single digital finite element model. Self-compacting concrete was essential in realising this geometry. The structural system essentially consists of 10 reinforced tapered concrete 'cones', rising from the basement car park to morph with, and support, a horizontal concrete floor slab. Each cone varies in form, plan geometry and height, with six cones entering into the main exhibition space and the remaining four continuing to support the steel roof structure. The cones convey the notion of dropped voids, which, in parts, provide additional floor space or act as access points to other floors. This provides a column-free space, creating a non-hierarchical system; not in terms of walls, slabs and columns, but instead shows the building structure as a whole entity. The first floor slab establishes changes in level by means of its waffle structure, which folds within a 900 mm deep zone, creating changes in density and seamlessly folding into the vertical cone structures.

The finish and compaction of the complex concrete geometries were enabled by the use of self-compacting concrete and specialist timber forms. Timber, polystyrene and metal forms were used to create forms to allow the cones to meet the floor with a flared geometry. A concrete mix without a superplastiser would not have allowed for adequate compaction, as the flow into the corners of the moulds would have been problematic and fitting vibrators up inside the shutters would have been time consuming and ineffective. This led to the use of self-compacting concrete, which was poured into the formwork in one continuous flow to prevent pour lines. Given the accelerated drying speed of self-compacting concrete, this had to be done quickly and efficiently to fill pours of up to 7 m high at 50 degrees from the vertical. Owing to the high volume of the pour, the shuttering was specially designed to account for increased pressure and the possibility of bleeding and concrete leaking from the shuttering.

> 'The design process was an intense collaboration of the Architectural and Structural disciplines made possible by the full use of drawing and analysis packages within the 3D environment.'
> *Project engineer Paul Scott of Adams Kara Taylor*[7]

2.22 Phaeno Science Centre, completed 2005
Designed by Zaha Hadid Architects; Engineer: Adams Kara Taylor

3.1 Pulitzer Foundation for the Arts – the concrete wall
adjacent to a sculpture by Richard Serra
Architect: Tadao Ando

THREE **in situ + precast**

'Concrete is a true structural material that represents its own time.
When constructed and maintained properly nothing can surpass concrete.'
Tadao Ando[1]

Having decided to design your project using concrete components, how do you determine whether you should cast the concrete on site (known as in situ) or use factory produced precast concrete? Both techniques can be an excellent method of delivering the benefits of concrete and often structures use in situ and precast concrete to combine the advantages of both techniques. These are described as hybrid concrete structures (HCS).

In situ concrete

The beauty of in situ concrete is its formability, which facilitates the creation of bespoke or one-off geometry that is design and site specific. In essence there is no limitation on dimensions, demonstrated by major site-cast civil engineering projects – such as the Hoover Dam (1931–36), the pylons of Le Viaduc de Millau (1993–2004; architects Foster and Partners with Chapelet-Defol-Mousseigne), or the power-floated floors of a large industrial building, for example the Renault Centre, Swindon (1980–82; architects Foster Associates). This technique was also used on the Hongkong and Shanghai Bank Headquarters (1979–85). This project may not appear to be characterized by its use of concrete. However the largest floors were poured at rate of 1,800 m² square per day. The steel superstructure of the bank supports over 60,000 m² of in situ concrete.[2]

3.2 Hoover Dam, 1931–36, in the Black Canyon of the Colorado River
Built by Six Companies Inc.

Thus, the concrete in the superstructure of the bank represents about 34 pours of concrete.

The advantages of in situ concrete are that:

- flexible site-based processes and complex forms can be readily achieved;
- small-scale to very large-scale structures can be created;
- it is a locally based industry in the UK;
- ready-mix industry can provide batching of the mix – sand, aggregates and cement – providing consistent colour and dependable performance characteristics;

3.3   Le Viaduc de Millau
Architect: Foster and Partners with Chapelet-Defol-Mousseigne

- large volumes of concrete can be safely pumped into the formwork;
- repetitive and reusable formwork is now common;
- there are a wide range of finishes;
- it allows the integration of details and services; and
- post-tensioning is an option.

The production of in situ concrete, however, does have limitations, including:

- the tolerances of in situ concrete need to be well understood in detail, as well as other elements that need to interface with the concrete;
- in situ concrete needs to be protected in very cold weather, below -0°C, to guard against frost damage;
- care needs to be taken to avoid excessive blow holes in exposed concrete which is visually important, and this is limited by BS 8500-1: 2006, *Concrete*;

3.4   Pouring of the reinforced concrete slab on the Hongkong and Shanghai Bank, 28 March 1984
Architect: Foster and Partners

- services need to be carefully integrated at the design stage; and
- the structural strength of the concrete should be checked via cube test to BS 8500-1: 2006, *Concrete*.

Key terms

FORMWORK

A structure, usually temporary, used to contain poured concrete to mould it to the required dimensions and to support it until it is able to support itself. It consists primarily of the face contact material and the bearers that directly support the face contact material.[3]

SHUTTERING

An alternative term for formwork.

FALSEWORK

Any temporary structure used to support a permanent structure until it is self-supporting.[4]

POUR

The amount of concrete that is placed in a single activity before it sets.

POWER FLOATING

The creation of a flat and smooth top surface to in situ concrete slabs by mechanical means.

A full glossary of the key terms used in the production and placement of concrete can be found at: www.ribabookshops.com/concreteglossary

3.5   The starter bars in the reinforced in situ concrete of a cone during the construction of the Phaeno Science Centre – awaiting shuttering for the next day's pour or lift

The other primary advantage of in situ concrete is that it is simple to produce monolithic structures; this is readily achieved by leaving the reinforcement exposed between pours of the concrete, which are known as starter bars and to which the next section of reinforcement can be attached, the shutter being secured to the earlier section of concrete. The joints formed are called cold joints or day work joints.

Paul Scott of Adams Kara Taylor, engineer for the Phaeno Science Centre, when challenged to explain the strength of reinforced concrete in 'human terminology' replied:

'If you consider a reinforced concrete wall 300 mm thick in a one metre by one metre square on elevation there would be 33–40 kg of steel reinforcement embedded within that square metre (which is equivalent to about half the body weight of a person in steel). The concrete surrounding that steel would weigh about 650 kg (which is equivalent to the weight of about 8– 9 persons).

The theoretical capacity of this wall in terms of supporting vertical load is

3.6   A plastic spacer that sets out the correct
cover – photographed at Canal Street,
Nottingham

about 450 tonnes (which is equivalent
to about 300 family cars). Although in
reality the wall will also be required to
work in bending as well as supporting
axial loads so its vertical load capacity
will be less.'[5]

The key to producing durable concrete is careful
detailing and placement of the reinforcement.
It is essential when using high-tensile steel to
achieve adequate coverage from the reinforcement and this is dependent on the exposure of
the site and is set out in BS 8500-1: 2006,
Concrete. Reinforcement is designed not only
to take the primary tensile loads, but also to
minimise any chance cracking. This is crucial
in avoiding potential structural failure when
concrete is exposed to the elements and to
ingress of water. Typically, a two-directional
steel mesh is used to prevent cracking in
the slab and wall sections. Reinforcement is
designed not only to take the primary tensile
loads, but also to minimise any cracking.

The key to producing durable concrete is
the careful detailing and placement of the
reinforcement and achieving a robust concrete
mix suited to the particular environment.
It is essential when using high-tensile
steel reinforcing bars to place them in the
formwork with sufficient concrete cover to
avoid corrosion of the reinforcement in the

lifetime of the structure. Initially, reinforcement
inside concrete is protected from corrosion,
however, the ingress of CO_2, or marine or
de-icing salts, will eventually result in the
reinforcement corroding. With the passage
of time, the corrosion, which is an expansive
reaction, causes 'spalling' – the popping
off of the concrete outer-layer, exposing the
reinforcement. A range of spacers have been
developed to aid in the placement of the
reinforcing bars, seeking to ensure that a
correct cover is achieved, and these range from
ceramic spacers, which can be colour matched
to the concrete, to plastic spacers, as shown in
Figure 3.6.

The structure of the Palazzo dello Sport,
by Pier Luigi Nervi, is monolithic in situ
concrete cast on ferro cement pans or
formwork. Nervi used ferro cement for the
accuracy that was essential in the delivery of
this dome with its delicate radiated geometry.
Thomas W. Leslie, in his essay 'Form as
Diagram of Forces: The Equiangular Spiral in
the Work of Pier Luigi Nervi',[6] describes the
project thus:

> 'The best known of Nervi's rotated
> lamella domes is the small Olympic
> arena built for the 1960 games in
> Rome. While the larger indoor space,
> the Palazzo dello Sport, consisted of a
> prefabricated trough system, analogous
> to the first Turin Exhibition Hall
> structure composed on a polar grid,
> the Palazzetto dello Sport represented
> the purest realization of the radial pan
> system. From the outside, the overall
> structural action of the dome is clearly
> expressed.'

The diamond forms of the lamella are
proportional, allowing a singular set of jigs
to manufacture the proportionally progressive
formwork. The angles of all the diamonds are
the same, it is only the lengths of the sides
that vary to generate each ring, as shown in
Figure 3.8.

3.7 The Palazzo dello Sport, Rome, under construction
Engineer: Pier Luigi Nervi

3.8 Thomas W. Leslie's analysis of Pier Luigi Nervi's geometry
of the dome of the Palazzo dello Sport

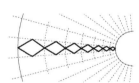

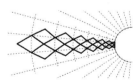

Typically the most time-consuming part
of building with in situ concrete is the
construction of the shuttering or formwork on
site. The time associated with the construction
of formwork can be reduced by the reuse of
shuttering and this has led to the development
of repetitive formwork techniques, which
include tunnel form and progressive formwork
techniques, such as slip form. These are
reviewed in more detail in Chapter 4, showing
how vital formwork is to the 'as struck' details
of concrete. If time is of the essence, then it is
better to specify precast concrete.

3.9   Transportation to site of a precast concrete T-beam

Precast concrete

This is a well-established modern method of construction, delivering robust components via offsite manufacturing. The advantages of precast concrete arise from fabricating components in factory conditions and include:

- excellent quality control;
- precision moulds – a close control of tolerances;
- a wide range of fine finishes;
- crisp edge details;
- batching of sand, aggregates and cement – providing consistent colour and dependable performance characteristics;
- the integration of details and services;
- pre-tensioning; and
- large components which are simple and rapid to install.

The production of precast concrete, however, does have limitations, including:

- the transportation of heavy components;
- the size and shape of components can also be limited by transportation;
- the form of the precast component needs to be strickable (i.e. can you get it out of the mould?); and
- the need for repetition to amortise or limit the impact of the cost of the mould.

The maximum size of a precast component will be limited by the road transport regulations and the specific location of the site, for example the presence of a low bridge on the route to the site. However, very large components can be transported. In the UK a load of over 25.9 m long by up to 4.5 m high, and over 4.3 m wide, requires both notice to the police and a 'vehicle mate', in accordance with Road Vehicles (Construction and Use) Regulations. It is possible to transport very long loads, subject to verification of the complete route from factory

3.10 Transportation to site of the precast concrete sections of Ballingdon Bridge
Designed by Michael Stacey Architects

3.11 Support over the River Stour of the pier foot of Ballingdon Bridge

to site; T-beam bridge sections of over 75 m have been transported to site (this is a common size for T-beam bridges in the USA) – essentially the T-beam becomes the chassis of the lorry, as shown in Figure 3.9. The typical component miles or delivery distance of a precast concrete component in Britain is 100 miles.[7]

The loads exerted on the precast concrete elements during transportation and erection need to be carefully considered at an early stage. The curvilinear components of Ballingdon Bridge were supported on mild steel cradles, which also formed part of the temporary construction. Stainless steel fixing points were integrated into the bridge section to accept the fixings of these temporary supports. In a precast concrete cladding panel, often the fixing details will also act as the points for lifting and temporary support.

For each precast manufacture there is an optimum utilisation of each mould. A single wooden mould can be typically used to cast about 30 units before repairs will be necessary. To speed up the production process, the precaster will use additives in the mix to speed up the curing process, typically striking moulds in a 24-hour cycle. Therefore, if cost of the component is critical, there is a need to achieve good repetition. The diagram in Figure 3.12 shows Trent Concrete's analysis of the

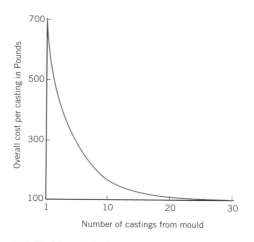

3.12 Trent Concrete's diagram on repetition – economy of production is achieved if the mould can be reused to produce at least 25 units

repetition of units and how this reduces the cost by spreading the cost of the mould over a large number of units. The life of a mould is dependent on whether it is made from wood, polymer composite or steel. On a large project it may be necessary to have more than one mould for the same component – this may be due to wear, or the need to deliver all of the components within a given construction programme.

3.13 The new synagogue in Desden, completed 2001
Architect: Wandel Hoefer Lorch & Hirsch

3.14 The gently spiral planes of the façade of the synagogue

3.15 The corbelled precast concrete blocks of the synagogue

Precast concrete is often selected for its robustness and the high quality of finish. Perhaps the term 'artificial stone' is more than simply a marketing label, it reveals the mimetic origins of precast concrete and the quality that can be produced. The new synagogue in Dresden, designed by Wandel Hoefer Lorch and Hirsch and constructed in 2001, replaces Gottfried Semper's earlier synagogue of 1840, which was destroyed by fire in 1938. In an act of constructional continuity, the closed monolithic form and cubic space of this new place of worship make direct reference to the Temple of Solomon on Mount Zion. The site of Semper's synagogue is kept empty, forming a courtyard between the community hall and the new synagogue. The façades of the synagogue are constructed from sandstone-like precast concrete blocks, which measure 1,200 mm by 600 mm by 600 mm. The blocks were precast in steel moulds, in Belgium, using a mix of yellow Bayer pigment, white and Portland cement, sand, quartz and yellow limestone aggregate. The site placement of the synagogue has a shifted alignment that is resolved by the blocks of the courtyard façade being stepped out or corbelled at each course forming a gentle spiral, with the top of the façade facing due east. The façade is corbelled by a total of 1,800 mm. Architect of the synagogue, Nikolaus Hirsh, stated:

> 'The precast stone that we chose does respond to the historic buildings of the old city and also echoes the prefabricated concrete of the apartment blocks of the 1960s and 1970s close by. Precast concrete as artificial stone bridges both urban contexts.'[8]

The textile laboratories of the Expertex Textile Centrum, designed by Brookes Stacey Randall and IAA Architecten, used precast concrete for its economy and as a key compositional element of the design, using the repetition of identical grey Portland cement based precast units. The design of the laboratory façades uses repetition within a coordinated module to articulate the laboratory spaces within this new facility for TNO. Although the architects of the Expertex Textile Centrum designed in the use of precast concrete for the cowls of the laboratory windows and the south-west end elevation of the building, which is in essence a large-scale

3.16 The Expertex Textile
Centrum used precast
concrete for its economy.
The repetition of the
identical window cowls
is a key part of the
architectural expression of
this project
Architect: Brookes Stacey
Randall and IAA Architecten

3.17 Expertex Textile Centrum – the new laboratories in elevation
with the original textile school building behind

3.18 Detail of the south-west facing elevation of the Expertex
Textile Centrum laboratory block – stainless steel woven mesh,
tensioned back to a precast concrete cowel

reprise of the repeated window cowel, the
contractor also proposed the use of precast
concrete for the walls too. The building had
been designed with exposed concrete surfaces
in order to maximise the available thermal
mass and was tendered on the basis that the
internal wall would be fair-faced

in situ concrete, but this was changed to
precast concrete as the main contractor offered
a significant saving in time and capital cost.

As discussed above, precast concrete is at its
most cost effective if the moulds can be used
many times, amortizing the cost of the mould

3.19 Stop moulds at Trent Concrete

across say 25–30 components. The need to reuse moulds, however, is not a restraint on the imagination of an architect. It is possible to provide a family of elements that come from the same mould by using stop sections and inserts. For example, symmetrical panels can be produced with left- and right-hand variants – this is clearly demonstrated on the cladding of the Experian Data Centre, Nottingham, for architects Shepherd Robson, where Trent Concrete produced a family of panel variants using stop sections in a common mould. It is essential in the design of a precast concrete component that the form can be removed from the mould – thus draft angles should be included and under cuts need to be avoided. Imagine how the precast component can be withdrawn from the mould. Early consultation with specialist subcontractors is strongly recommended.

Often projects are not as standardised as they appear, a set of cladding panels can appear to be identical with the same overall module and window arrangement, yet the precast manufacture has integrated a range of details, services and components into the panels, creating a range of variants.

A key advantage of the use of precast concrete is the short time needed for installation. It is one of the established modes of prefabrication. Early interaction with the precast supplier is essential, and this can modify the design process in the architect's and engineer's offices. It is critical to establish fixing and other interface details at the earliest opportunity as this will influence the detailing of the precast concrete and other elements that interface with it – in cladding this is typically the steel or concrete frame of the building. Detailing these interfaces at the earliest possible stage can generate significant savings. Many precast suppliers are willing to work with architects at an early stage of the project to provide their specialist knowledge to the design team. A very good way of achieving this is by using a partnering contract, where no one in the construction team is asked to work at risk. It is vital that details and interfaces are resolved at an early stage. One benefit of prefabrication is that it reduces the overall delivery period for a project, thus minimising the economic risks to the client, while providing more 'thinking time' for the design team. In construction, spending time during the design to think through all the aspects of the project is cost-effective – as people, machinery and materials have not yet been committed to site.

The plasticity of concrete means it can be readily used to make highly integrated components. The precast concrete units of the Toyota Headquarters' Building (architect Shepherd Robson) each integrate the air-handling duct work and the services for lighting into the precast component, providing a smooth curvilinear soffit, essential for the fabric storage of heat and lighting, uninterrupted by the need for other elements. This is an added value component that undertakes a number of roles integrated into a single component, thus minimising the overall cost of construction. In essence, this is an adaptation of lean manufacturing techniques from the automobile industry – it is better and quicker to install, and more reliable and cheaper to use one component rather than, say, four. Appropriately, for this project, the concept of lean manufacturing itself was pioneered by Taiichii Ohno of Toyota in the second half of the twentieth century.

Increasingly, architects and engineers are combining the advantages of precast and in situ concrete to create hybrid structures. The Headquarters of Toyota (GB) is an excellent example of a hybrid structure. The soffit comprises precast concrete units manufactured using a limestone from Derbyshire and a white cement to produce an exposed near white

3.20 Highly integrated components incorporating air handling, manufactured in white precast concrete floor slabs for the Headquarters of Toyota (GB) at Trent Concrete

3.21 The precast concrete soffit of the Headquarters of Toyota (GB)
Architect: Shepherd Robson

soffit, which is important for the day and artificial lighting of the offices. As stated above, the panels integrate services for lighting and extract ducts, while forming a vital part of the interior architecture, and they provide exposed thermal mass as part of a fabric storage strategy. There are four office wings, each 15 m wide, and the office wings have a 9 m x 7.5 m column grid and each floor plate comprises 34 panels, which are 6 m x 3 m. The precast concrete provides the fine finish and integrated detailing, the in situ slab and up stand provide structural continuity and create a monolithic structure. This approach provides a combination of a short construction time, a high visual quality and a holistic approach to the architecture, creating a well-tempered space in which people can work productively. For a review of detailed research into hybrid concrete structure funded by the Department for Trade and Industry (DTI) see *Best Practice Guidance for Hybrid Concrete Construction* by C. H. Goodchild and J. Glass.[9]

At the Powergen Operational Headquarters, designed by Bennetts Associates, the contractor Laing decided to cast the exposed concrete floor sections using glass fibre polyester moulds. However, in order to minimise transportation costs, the sections were precast on site and were craned into position, in essence creating a one-off site-based factory. The Powergen Operational Headquarters is the first large-scale demonstration of the benefits of using internally exposed concrete as thermal mass to provide fabric energy storage for a contemporary office building and, thus, passively moderating the internal temperature – see Chapter 10 for details of this technique.

3.22 Powergen Operational Headquarters
Architect: Bennetts Associates

3.23 Placing the reinforcement cages of the concrete floors of the Powergen Operational Headquarters over the curvilinear precast soffit units

facing page
3.24 The internally exposed concrete frame of the Powergen Operational Headquarters viewed from the atrium

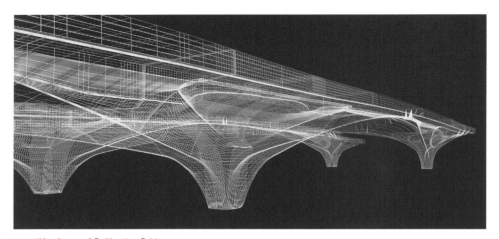

3.25 Wire frame of Ballingdon Bridge,
developed by Michael Stacey Architects

Ballingdon Bridge

The setting in Suffolk is a wonderful combination of water meadows that surround Sudbury and the listed buildings that form a conservation area. There have been bridges on this site, crossing the Stour, since the twelfth century. The new Ballingdon Bridge is an integral reinforced concrete structure that carries the A131 over the River Stour. The previous bridge, built in 1911, was not capable of sustaining heavy traffic, including 42-tonne articulated lorries, and a closure would have resulted in a 35-mile diversion off this trunk road.

The new bridge was designed to be visually calm while respecting the historic context and providing an urban design, which remains focused on All Saints Church and the diverse geometry of the listed buildings of Ballingdon village. The structure, however, has a dynamically three-dimensional soffit. Designed by Michael Stacey Architects using an evolutionary digital technique, the bridge has an ever changing and site-specific geometry that fulfils the complex functional and cultural requirements of the project.[10] 'The design for Ballingdon Bridge has a gently curvilinear profile and a dynamically morphed soffit. Within this ever-changing geometry no two adjacent sections are the same. It was designed using an iterative lofting technique. The geometry morphs from slice to slice and at the pier feet the architect prepared sections at 47 mm centres, a section under every 2 inches.'[11] The feet of the new bridge appear to lightly touch the surface of the water. A key aim for the architect was to uphold the rich architectural traditions and construction quality of Suffolk. Sudbury was the home of Gainsborough and the landscape of the

3.26 Ballingdon Bridge at night, illustrating integrated lighting in the scoops
Designed by Michael Stacey Architects; Engineers Ove Arup & Partners

River Stour is set in Constable country. The bridge fully utilises the beauty, plasticity and expressive quality of concrete.

The project was specified and constructed on a sustainable basis; the earlier bridge was recycled and the wildlife and river environment were carefully protected during the construction. The new bridge incorporates bat boxes and an otter run. The bats need the darkness under the bridge and the otters are afraid of it. The bridge has also been designed to minimise the risk of flooding, acting as a dam and thus protecting local properties.

Developing the design, following the RIBA design competition, involved extensive consultation with stakeholders and the people of Sudbury and Ballingdon. Delivering the design took close collaboration and teamwork, facilitated by partnering. The construction of the bridge was undertaken on a partnering

basis using a New Engineering Contract (NEC) partnering contract (NEC Option C: Target contract with activity schedule). By careful study of the construction and phasing of the bridge, as well as extensive prefabrication, disruption to Ballingdon was minimised and traffic flow across the bridge was maximised during reconstruction. The bridge was rebuilt in 18 months and has a design life of 120 years.

All the materials of the new bridge were carefully selected to respond to the local context and to fulfil the performance requirement of a road bridge, combining engineering, urban design and architecture. The materials palette was discussed in detail with the planning officer. For example, the mix for the precast concrete was selected to match the local limestone of the twelfth-century Norman church.

3.27 Digital design and craftsmanship combined to create the timber moulds of Ballingdon Bridge

The precast units were manufactured by Buchan in timber models, which were beautifully crafted from the architect's digital geometry. Buchan combined civil engineering scale of components; the bridge pier units weighed 26 tonne with a fine architectural finish. This, in part, was made possible by the sophisticated batching technology of Buchan's Accrington factory, maintaining a consistent mix throughout the 12 precast units of the bridge structure. The mix was based on a white Portland cement produced by Castle Cement in Ketton and 14 mm single-size coarse aggregate and fine aggregate, all from Ballidon in Debryshire. It had a

3.28 Pier foot mould of Ballingdon Bridge, at Buchan's works in Accrington

3.29 The 26-tonne precast concrete pier foot unit of Ballingdon Bridge being craned out of its mould

3.30 A pier foot unit of Ballingdon Bridge being craned into position on site in Suffolk

3.31 The in situ slab of Ballingdon Bridge that ties all the precast concrete units together forming a monolithic structure – note the incorporation of bat boxes

cement content of 440 kg/m^3 and a Sika superplasticiser to produce a high workability with a dense and low-permeability finish. The moulds were struck after 48 hours and the units lifted out; at this stage the test cubes had reached 35 Mpa (35 N/mm^2). After 28 days, test cubes were measured at 60 Mpa. The carefully selected palette of materials also included granite, stainless steel, aluminium and English oak. Even the aggregate within the tarmac was agreed with the planning officer.

Michael Stacey, the partner in charge of Ballingdon Bridge, observed, in *AD Special Edition: Design Through Making*, that it is possible to combine fast construction and slow architecture: 'It is now possible to combine robust, rapidly deployable contemporary technology, and the immutable qualities of architecture to create slow architecture ... an architecture of the finest ingredients designed to be purposeful, savoured and enjoyed',[12] yet constructed in the shortest possible time. Ballingdon Bridge was rebuilt in just 18 months while keeping the traffic flowing and protecting the environment of the River Stour.

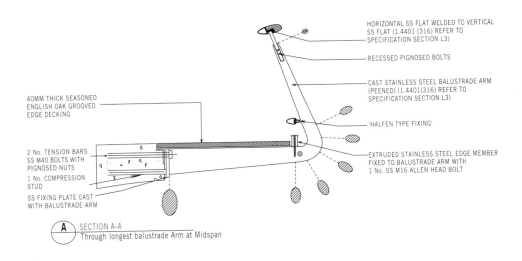

HORIZONTAL SS FLAT WELDED TO VERTICAL
SS FLAT (1.4401 (316) REFER TO
SPECIFICATION SECTION L3)

RECESSED PIGNOSED BOLTS

CAST STAINLESS STEEL BALUSTRADE ARM
(PEENED) (1.4401(316) REFER TO
SPECIFICATION SECTION L3)

'HALFEN TYPE FIXING'

EXTRUDED STAINLESS STEEL EDGE MEMBER
FIXED TO BALUSTRADE ARM WITH
1 No. SS M16 ALLEN HEAD BOLT

40MM THICK SEASONED
ENGLISH OAK GROOVED
EDGE DECKING

2 No. TENSION BARS
SS M40 BOLTS WITH
PIGNOSED NUTS

1 No. COMPRESSION
STUD

SS FIXING PLATE CAST
WITH BALUSTRADE ARM

A) SECTION A-A
Through longest balustrade Arm at Midspan

3.32 Architect's detailed drawing of the balustrade system for Ballingdon Bridge

The balustrade has been designed to be visually open so that the views of the landscape are as uninterrupted as possible. This 'P2 Low Containment' balustrade, in combination with the bollards, is capable of arresting a 42 tonne truck, yet appears to be an elegant pedestrian handrail. The traffic and pedestrian functions of the bridge have been safely separated, the pavement being protected by bollards, which also house light fittings. This safety system was designed specifically for the bridge. The visually open, yet robust, balustrade was achieved by a combination of purpose-made extruded aluminium sections, stainless steel wires and stainless steel castings. In the event of a vehicle colliding with the balustrades, the bolts fixing the castings have been designed to shear off before the precast concrete is damaged.

3.33 Ballingdon Bridge crossing the River Stour, Suffolk

On impact, all the components work together to form a 'ribbon' that will arrest the vehicle. The top rail is a combination of extruded aluminium and English oak. This point of human contact is key to the design; to a pedestrian, the vehicular safety role is intended to be an unseen quality. The enlarged walkways create a generous provision for pedestrians to enjoy the views of the river and meadows. People enjoying the river and the urban spaces of Sudbury are the priority within the design of this road bridge. The contribution of this bridge to Constable country has been recognised by national and international awards, including an award from the Campaign for the Preservation of Rural England.

4.1   The in situ concrete slab under construction
      at Indescon Court, London, E14, showing
      the textile quality of the reinforcing mesh

formwork + finishes

'But although no visible "powers of design" from inside the concrete conglomerate penetrate the thin outer layer, the surface still exhibits texture – traces of a structure that no longer exists: the formwork. All that can still be detected on exposed concrete are "fingerprints". The term "texture" stems from the same origin as "text" or "textile" – meaning fabric – and thus immediately hints at what earlier on has been dubbed "filigree construction".'
Andrea Deplazes [1]

Formwork is the essential precursor of in situ concrete. It is either temporary or permanent. Temporary formwork can be categorised in two ways: site constructed, typically timber-based systems, with little or no potential for reuse as shuttering; or engineered formwork, typically prefabricated off site, which, depending on the choice of shuttering finish, may be reused a significant number of times. The potential exists for temporary formwork to be reused, as something other than shuttering, as part of the complete construction as demonstrated by the Ceramics Studio and Store in Hagi, Japan (designed by Sambuichi Architects), which is discussed and illustrated on pages 79–81. Permanent formwork can also be categorised in two ways: hollow pre-formed blocks of materials, such as fibre cement or polystyrene, which are laid as a blockwork wall, with concrete poured into the cavity in stages; or pre-formed panels of materials, such as fibre cement, reinforced-plastic, textiles, steel or precast concrete, which are simply left as the surface once the concrete has cured and the falsework is removed.

The design of formwork itself is typically the responsibility of the contractor, with the architect and engineer responsible for specifying the end product of the transitory formwork. For instance, Tadao Ando's bolthole arrangements are generally designed for visual consistency, with false boltholes added to the formwork in the areas where ties are mechanically unnecessary. In the case of permanent formwork, the architect should be more concerned with the design. It may also be necessary for the architect or engineer to design formwork in order to consider its influence upon the overall design of more complex structures. While contractors may often be best suited for the design of formwork, by negating responsibility over this area, the architect loses control over a significant proportion of the material, time, energy and cost required to produce a concrete structure. Care should also be taken in making certain that all timber used on site is from a certified renewal source,

Lap – fins can form

Tongue and groove – grout tight formwork, reuse is difficult

V-groove – fins can form

Undercut lap – grout tight formwork, readily reused

Butt – fins can form [2]

4.2   Methods of joining shuttering sheets

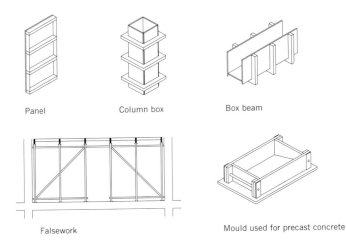

Panel   Column box   Box beam

Falsework   Mould used for precast concrete

4.3   Primary types of formwork

4.4   Smooth concrete external walls – Hepworth
Museum, Wakefield, under construction.
It will open in the Spring of 2011
Architect: David Chipperfield

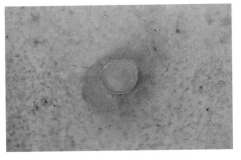

4.5   Smooth in situ pigmented dark grey self
compacting concrete external walls cast with
Wisa® Form BETO faces to the formwork, this is a
thermoplastic coated birch plywood.

such as the Forestry Stewardship Council, even
the timber purchased by the contractor for
temporary works, including shuttering. Exposed
concrete requires the careful coordination of
the shuttering sizes, fixing method and the
integration of services.

Formwork and accuracy of construction

Understanding the potential accuracy of the
chosen type of concrete and the prevailing
national standards is a vital starting point for

architecture based on the use of concrete.
Forming an appreciation of the cultural
context and the potential cost of achieving
fine tolerances is a critical thought process for
a project that uses concrete. The placement
tolerances for in situ shuttering can be
found in the *National Structural Concrete
Specification* (NSCS).[3] The specifying architect
may state a higher standard in the project
specification or possible switch into the use
of precast concrete. To achieve the quality of
smooth shuttered in situ concrete required by

DK Tie system
1. Spacer Tube Rough (x1)
2. DK Sealing Cone (x2)
3. DK Concrete Cone (x2)

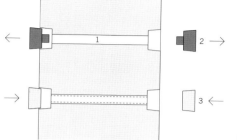

4.6   Lost formwork tie rod drawing and components, courtesy of Peri

SK Tie system
1. Lost tie rod (x1)
2. SK Tie Cone (x2)
3. SK Concrete Cone (x2)

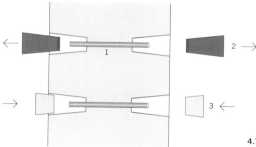

4.7   Spacer tube formwork tie: drawing and components, courtesy of Peri

4.8   Examples of precast concrete cones

4.9   Nervi's use of ferro cement formwork on the
Palazzo dello Sport, with the in situ concrete
triangular ring beam yet to be clad

David Chipperfield Architects on the Hepworth
Museum, asked the main contractor to agree to
a tolerance between shutter boards of ± 3 mm
where the standard tolerance would have been
± 5 mm. Earlier areas of wall that were outside
the agreed tolerance range were demolished.
This attention to detail drove the fabrication of
the formwork and contributed to the fine finish
achieved, as shown in Figure 4.60. Whereas
to achieve the geometric precision needed to
build the dome of the Palazzo dello Sport,

Pier Luigi Nervi used ferro cement formwork.
In essence he used the precision of a precast
factory product to control the geometry of this
in situ concrete structure.

Reusable formwork
Site-built formwork can be up to 40% of the
cost of concrete construction. To reduce this
cost, a wide range of fully reusable formwork
systems have been developed, from wall
panel systems to aluminium framed table-like

4.10 Wall panel shuttering system with the concrete being placed from a hopper

4.11 Prefabricated aluminium framed table formwork, which is also known as flying formwork

4.12 Aluminium framed table formwork ready for the next floor slab, on site at Canal Street, Nottingham

formwork for the repetitive castings of slabs. These systems reduce the embodied energy of the concrete as they can be reused on many projects. Table formwork is also described as flying formwork, which can be readily understood by viewing Figure 4.11. These systems are struck and reused lift-by-lift or floor-by-floor. For repetitive cellular geometries, tunnel formwork could prove to be the best option. For tall structures, two options have been developed to speed up the construction process and reduce waste: climbing formwork and slip form.

Climbing formwork
These are constructed in regular consecutive lifts, supported by the previous hardened lift of concrete. Formwork may be struck without being fully dismantled and then raised for the

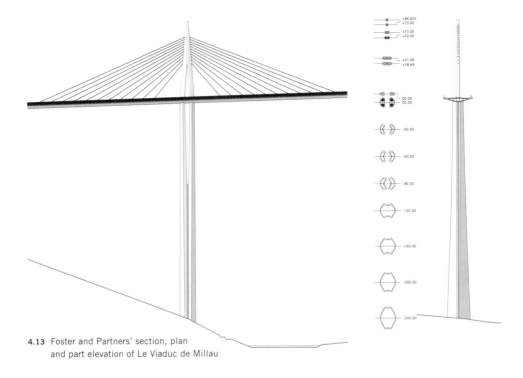

4.13 Foster and Partners' section, plan and part elevation of Le Viaduc de Millau

next lift. The upper tie holes from the previous lift become the fixing for the lower tie holes of the following lift. The reinforced concrete pylons of Le Viaduc de Millau were cast using Peri climbing formwork. The pylons have a sectional geometry that changes as they rise up. The formwork comprised purpose-made steel shuttering to produce a high quality of concrete. The concrete was cast on a three-day cycle and the formwork rose hydraulically. In total there are seven pylons with heights that range between 78 m and 245 m, enabling this motorway bridge to cross the River Tarn valley in southern France. The 90-m high superstructure of the bridge was fabricated

4.14 The concrete pylons of Le Viaduc de Millau were cast using steel-faced Peri climbing formwork

4.15 Emley Moor Transmission Mast, completed 1970
Designed by Ove Arup and Partners

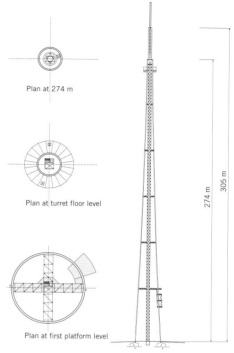

Plan at 274 m

Plan at turret floor level

Plan at first platform level

305 m

274 m

4.16 A vertical section and key plans through the
Emley Moor Transmission Mast

from steel. Le Viaduc de Millau was designed by Foster and Partners in collaboration with Chapelet-Defol-Mousseigne, and the engineering was undertaken by Setra led by Michael Virlogeux. Other consultants included EEG (Europe Etudes Gecti), Sogelerg, SERF and Agence TER.

An earlier example of the use of climbing formwork is the Emley Moor Transmission Mast that was designed by Ove Arup & Partners and completed in 1970. This mast remains the UK's tallest freestanding structure at 330 m high. The need for a new mast resulted from the collapse of the previous steel mast on 19 March 1969. The new mast was transmitting again within 22 months. This was achieved by the use of climbing formwork. The concrete

structure of the mast was cast in 122 lifts in 44 weeks by Tileman & Co. Bartak and Shears recorded that 'the highest rate of casting achieved being five lifts per week'.[4] The primary superstructure of the mast is a tapering tubular concrete shell, which is 274.32 m high. At the base it is 24.38 m in diameter, with a wall thickness of 533 mm – this reduces to a diameter of 6.4 m at the top, where the wall thickness is only 350 mm. Welding four of the vertical reinforcing rods at each lift provides a key part of the lightning protection of the mast. A glass-fibre reinforced plastic (GRP) clad lattice steel tower 50.08 m high completes the mast.

A total of 7,000 m³ of concrete, with a minimum strength of 40 MPa (40 N/mm²) was used to form the shell structure, combined with 660 tonnes of steel reinforcement. It was cast in 2.3 m lifts using specially developed steel shutters. The external shutter comprised a set of overlapping steel plates that were tensioned together; the internal shutter was sprung outwards. Minor changes in taper and diameter were facilitated by the overlapping plates, which where interchanged when required by the diminishing setting out geometry.

Slip formwork
These are raised continuously, unlike climbing forms, slowly sliding against the fresh concrete to form a monolithic structure without joints. This requires a uniform cross-section of the entire lift in order to allow continuous progression of the formwork. Work must progress 24 hours a day, with duplication of all necessary equipment to allow for the continuous construction in the event of any failures. For this reason, the height of the structure should be at least 20 m in order to offset the equipment costs.

Tunnel formwork
This moveable formwork is suitable for repetitive cellular large cross-wall structures and can typically form cells or rooms with spans between 2.4 m and 6.6 m, and thus is ideal in forming the primary structure for housing or hotels. Tunnels consist of two braced 'L' sections that rest upon the concrete of the previous lift. Tunnels are raised every 24 hours to the successive storey, providing a rapid method of construction. Tunnel form has also been used to form engineering structures, such as road and rail bridges. Architects Stephenson Bell have used tunnel form to construct the structure of a hotel that is part of the conversion and extension of Manchester's Free Trade Hall (see *Concrete Quarterly* 211 for further information on this project).[5]

What do you call building quickly?

We call it two big flats per day

4.17 *What do you call building quickly?*
An advertisement for tunnel formwork from *Industrialised Building: System and Components*, 5 (10), October 1968

4.18 Tunnel formwork under construction

4.19 Tunnel formwork being used to form the concrete structure of Queen Mary student accommodation for the University of London
Architect: Feilden Clegg Bradley Studio

Flexible fabric formwork

Flexible fabric formwork is a method of creating complex concrete forms that would otherwise be difficult and expensive to manufacture using conventional formwork systems. A number of universities, including Edinburgh and East London, are investigating the potential feasibility of fabric-cast concrete as a means of creating unique structural components. This research is being led by Remo Predreschi and Alan Chandler. The earliest use of fabric-cast concrete, however, was by Felix Candela in the 1950s. He used a timber framework draped in sackcloth to construct shell structures. In the 1970s, Miguel Fisac developed this idea through the exploration of sculptural fabric

4.20 Fabric formwork of a concrete wall (Wall One) undertaken by architecture students of the University of Edinburgh and the University of East London under the guidance of Remo Predreschi and Alan Chandler

4.21 Wall One produced using fabric formwork at the University of East London

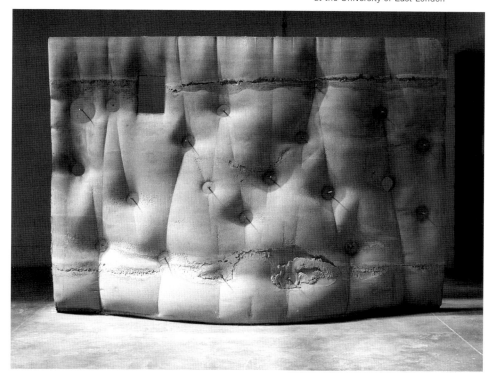

precast concrete panels. A key Canadian pioneer of fabric formwork is Mark West, whose experiments in this field of construction date back to 1986. In 2003, Fernández-Galiano used flexible plastic supported by a wire framework to create patterns on the finish of concrete panels.

Fabric formwork can be an economical method of creating structurally efficient components such as beams, columns and walls. Due to its flexibility, it carries loads by tension and, therefore, the form of the concrete depends on the level of elasticity and pre-tensioning of the fabric, which allows it to adopt the most efficient geometry to carry the weight of the wet concrete. To produce a fabric-cast concrete panel, a woven fabric mould is stretched across a reusable steel or timber frame and is clamped in position using rods, which will create a dimpled effect in the concrete surface. The most difficult part of the process is controlling the fabric geometry and its deformation, once the wet concrete is poured, to achieve the desired shape.

Different types of fabric can be used, such as cotton, polyester, woven and non-woven; although non-woven fabric may not come away from the concrete as easily on setting. The decision will depend on the desired textural effect and budget. The porosity of the fabric makes it permeable to air and excess water. This aids compaction and, consequentially, increases the density of the resulting concrete surface. The permeability of the fabric also limits surface irregularities, since the surface finish follows the texture of the fabric and reduces the possibility of blowholes.

For more information on fabric shuttering see *Fabric Formwork* by Alan Chandler and Remo Predreschi.[6]

4.23 A concrete beam formed in response to the required mending moment diagram using the inherent quality of the fabric formwork at the University of Edinburgh

4.22 Base detail – showing the expressive potential of concrete cast in fabric formwork

The Tactility Factory

This research and development project led by Ruth Morrow and Trish Belford represents a different mode of integration of textiles and concrete. Primarily aimed at producing interior components, the textiles remain as permanent surface elements in the concrete, demonstrating a decorative sensibility that I think would delight William Morris. Their aim is to create innovative 'soft' building surfaces. This challenges the perception of textiles as the 'dressing' to a structure and instead integrates textile technologies into the production of building components. The softness, both visual and acoustic, can introduce warmth into an exposed concrete interior – retaining the benefits of exposed thermal mass, yet avoiding a too reverberant interior. Morrow and Belford have developed textile concrete processes which are inventive enough to warrant patent protection, and this includes their linen concrete process.

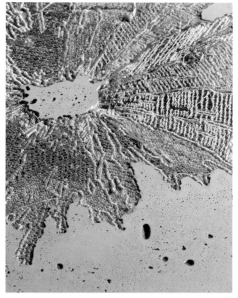

4.24 Stitched Concrete by Morrow and Belford, winner of the 2009 Multimedia Award in Royal Dublin Society's National Crafts Competition

4.25 A 7.5 m long frieze by Morrow and Belford installed in the refurbished Derry Playhouse during 2009

Permanent formwork

A method of avoiding the costs of temporary formwork is to incorporate the formwork into the final assembly. This may take the form of precast units used in hybrid construction. Careful consideration is required as typically permanent formwork remains visible in the final construction. The option is explored further in Chapter 6. Insulating permanent formwork systems have been developed to provide structural support for the concrete during hardening combined with effective thermal insulation.

Insulating concrete formwork (ICF) comprises a dry construction of lightweight hollow interlocking blocks of an insulating material, such as expanded polystyrene. Concrete is then poured into the cavity in progressive stages. The block forms remain in place to act as thermal insulation. In this method, materials and time can be saved by eliminating the investment in temporary formwork, while simultaneously providing insulation. Logix ICF has been used to form the basement of the first Creative Energy Home at the School of Architecture and the Built Environment at the University of Nottingham. Below ground the ICF walls are 298 mm thick and achieve a U-value of 0.2 W/m^2, and the structural core has been cast using a ggbs-based concrete.

BASF's Creative Energy Home, the second energy home built at the University of Nottingham, also uses ICF fabricated by Logix. To enhance the performance, the ICF uses Neopor®, an expanded polystyrene manufactured by BASF, and this incorporates graphite, hence the silver grey colour. More importantly, Neopor® achieves a better thermal performance than standard expanded polystyrene and it uses up to 50% less raw materials. However, in order to achieve a U-value of 0.15 W/m^2, an additional 55 mm thick layer of Neopor® was required, making the overall wall thickness 300 mm. Super-insulated ICF are now available, Logix produce a range of ICFs using Neopor with thickness up

4.26 The basement of the first Creative Energy Home formed of ICF

4.27 Students of the School of Architecture and the Built Environment, University of Nottingham, installing the reinforcing bars in the ICF ready for the pumping of the ggbs-based concrete, which forms the structural core

4.28 ICF forms the ground floor walls of BASF's Creative Energy Home, University of Nottingham

4.29 Pumping concrete into the insulating formwork on BASF's Creative Energy Home, University of Nottingham

to 356 mm and can provide ICFs with U-values as low as 0.075 W/m².

The concrete forming the core of the ICF was made pumpable by the addition of BASF's Rheocell admixture. This admixture also reduces the need for a fine aggregate, such as sand.

Lost formwork

The chapel sited in farmland near Waschendorf, Germany, is dedicated to a rural mystic Niklaus von Flüe (1417–1487) who was known as Brother Claus. It was built using what the architect Peter Zumthor describes as 'a rammed concrete' technique. A tower of slender tree trunks was erected, forming the core of a 12 m high tower, and the concrete was poured by 'farmers', 500 mm per day over 24 days. The timber was then burnt out, leaving a richly textured blackened interior. Although clearly contemporary, the chapel has raw and immutable qualities emphasised by an oculus that is open to the elements and a cast lead floor.

4.30 Bruder Klaus Kapelle (Brother Claus Chapel), completed in 2007
Architect: Peter Zumthor

4.31 The interior of Bruder Klaus Kapelle

Zumthor's architecture is characterised by his ability to turn the practical necessity of construction into a poetic set of possibilities that animate space with light. In the Bruder Klaus Kapelle the bolt holes that are essential to lock the two surfaces of the shuttering together and resist the bursting pressure of the wet concrete are expressed on the exterior, sleeved and caped internally with glass lenses. The tectonic expression of the blackened interior is animated by sparkling light.

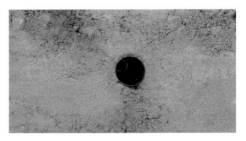

4.32 A shuttering bolthole in the 'rammed concrete' exterior of the Bruder Klaus Kapelle

Concrete finishes

For many architects the set of decisions on the finish and colour of concrete is the point at which the concrete becomes project specific and evident. Concrete can take on an extraordinary variety of finishes. It can be cast to be smooth, have a cast textured finish, or it can be post-treated to create a further array of textures. It is even possible to polish concrete after it has cured to create a marble-like, almost mirrored, appearance. The tectonic construction of temporary formwork can be expressed through the relief texture

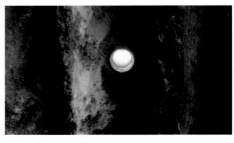

4.33 A lens set in the shuttering bolthole of the burnt out interior of the Bruder Klaus Kapelle

of the shuttering. In all cases concrete will inherently reflect the choice of formwork, except when extensively post-treated. Rough sawn pine, or spruce, is a common choice, leaving the impression of wood grain upon the concrete. The texture depends upon the wood's age, density and resin content, while the reuse of timber shuttering can cause the appearance to change, if the boards absorb water.

Post-treatment can be undertaken by physical or chemical means. This should be planned from the outset, as care needs to be taken to provide adequate distance between the treated concrete surface and the reinforcement, and in the choice of aggregate that will also become exposed, thus the colour of this aggregate becomes critical to the overall appearance of the concrete. The mechanical treatment of concrete is explored later in this chapter, for example see Figure 4.55, the Elephant and Rhino Pavilion at Regent's Park Zoo, London (architects Casson and Conder), and chemical treatment is explored via projects such as Eberswalde Library, designed by Herzog and de Meuron (see Figure 4.59).

As cast

The primary options for the finish of as cast concrete are dependent on the material selected for the face of the shutter:

- smooth sheets, for example steel, GRP or GRP face ply;
- rough sawn timber lining, typically pine or spruce;
- polymer lining, for example plastic film or cast silicone rubber; and
- corrugated or ribbed shutter, typically a moulded timber surface.

The decision to use a particular type of formwork can influence both the texture and colour of the concrete surface. The materials used to make different types of formwork will have varying levels of permeability. The more permeable the formwork, or the more absorbent

4.35 The atrium of the Royal Library Copenhagen has lyrical smooth-faced in situ concrete with expressed bolt holes
Architect: Schmidt Harmer Lassen

it is, will invariably have an impact on the surface colour of the concrete, as the water content of the mix near the surface is being modified by the face material of the formwork. An impermeable formwork with a shiny finish can cause discoloration to the concrete finish. Although impermeable forms are less likely to add unwanted colour to the surface of the concrete, they often create blowholes due to trapped air bubbles being unable to migrate through the formwork material. Permeability also determines the number of times the formwork can be reused. A totally impermeable formwork can be reused several hundred times, whereas a particularly permeable type may be used only once. Table 4.1 provides a guide to the selection of materials to form the shutter face.

Table 4.1: Guidance on the selection of materials to form the shutter face

Form-face type	Permeability	Effect on colour and texture	Blowholes/defects	Reuse
Steel (sheet or plate)	Completely impermeable	The shiny surface can leave a dark irregular colouring. Abrasive blast cleaning of the steel, prior to first use, can leave the concrete with a uniform light colouring. Creates a smooth surface texture	Blowholes are likely	Up to 500
Glass-fibre reinforced plastic (GRP)	Completely impermeable	Gives a smooth surface finish with a light colouring	Blowholes are likely	100 plus
All-birch plywood with a bonded phenolic resin film overlay (Heavy Duty Overlay or HDO)	Extremely low permeability	Gives a smooth surface finish, but can leave dark discolouration due to the shiny surface of the formwork. Staining is reduced when the surface gloss wears off after the first few uses	Blowholes are likely	50 plus
Douglas fir plywood with a resin-impregnated film overlay (Medium Duty Overlay or MDO)	Low permeability	Gives a more uniform surface colour than all the above forms. Dark lines may occur at unsealed edges where water has been absorbed by the formwork. Features in the wood may show through the MDO and leave imprints	Leaves fewer blowholes than all the above forms	10 to 20
Unsealed plywood (Finnish Birch, Douglas Fir, others)	Medium permeability	Dark patches may occur on the concrete where the wood has areas of high absorbency. This will become less after a few uses. The grain pattern will be visible	Few or no blowholes	10 to 20
Plain smooth timber boards (fir or spruce with planed surface)	Medium to high permeability	Board joints visible on the surface finish, grain pattern will show. Smooth surface with even colour distribution	Few or no blowholes	Up to 10
Rough timber boards (fir or spruce with rough sawn surface)	Medium to high permeability	Board joints visible on the surface finish, grain pattern will show. Even colour distribution. Irregular, but fine, textured surface finish	Few or no blowholes	4 to 5
Controlled permeability formwork (CPF) – micro-porous plastic sheet lining	Extremely high permeability due to fine pores permeable to water and air	A fine texture created by the CPF, and a dark colouring is left as the amount of surface water is reduced	Elimination of blowholes and surface water	Can be as few as 1

Smooth-faced shuttering

The smooth surface of concrete is a direct reflection of the material chosen as the face of the shuttering. Steel provides a smooth finish in a form that can be reused many times; the concrete blocks of the new synagogue in Dresden were precast in steel moulds (Figures 3.13–3.15) and the pylons of Le Viaduc de Millau were cast on site using steel shuttering (Figure 4.14). Typically, steel shuttering tends to produce a darker colour from a given mix, it can also result in blowholes in vertical surfaces. A cost-effective form of smooth-faced shuttering can be made using GRP-faced plywood. Smooth curvilinear forms, such as the floor slabs of the Powergen Operational Headquarters, are best cast onto GRP moulds (Figures 3.22–3.24). Smooth single curvature formwork can be readily created using birch ply formwork that has been pre-coated with a thermoplastic coating. This can be curved without fear of cracking the coating, which is typically 0.3 mm thick. UPM-Kymmone Wood provide such thermoplastic-coated curved plywood shuttering, including Wisa®Form

The triangular columns of Deodar, a house in Surrey designed by Eldridge Smerin, were cast in GRP-faced polystyrene Rapidobat® formwork, manufactured by H. Bau Technik. Although the columns are cast using a Portland cement based concrete, they have a reflective, almost marble-like, quality. Originally the soffit of this house was to be cast on a triangular grid, however, this was optimised to an orthogonal grid, as shown in Figure 4.37.

Rough sawn timber shutter lining

The plasticity of the concrete can be emphasised by the use of rough sawn timber as a lining to the shuttering, imparting into the concrete an echo of the material it was cast against. The walls of the National Theatre, London, designed by Dennis Lasdun, are a meticulously set out example of horizontal board marked concrete. This finish was chosen by Lasdun because the texture of the concrete emphasises the overall concept of the theatre

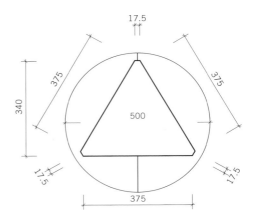

4.36 The shuttering general arrangement plan for the concrete columns of Deodar
Architect: Eldridge Smerin

4.37 The concrete frame of Deodar
Architect: Eldridge Smerin

building as a new layered landscape, a layered topography, on the banks of the Thames. In contrast, the waffle slab was cast with smooth GRP moulds.

The Kahn House is a refurbishment of an early Victorian north London terraced house by drdh architects. Over the years, the property had been significantly altered: a new storey had been added, the basement dug out, even

4.38 National Theatre, London
Architect: Dennis Lasdun

4.39 The board marked concrete of the National Theatre

4.40 A 1:10 cast plaster model of a waffle slab at the National Theatre made by Anna Crosby to study this structure and concrete casting methods (see also pages 134–135)

the corbelled foundations of the party walls had been cut off. The project grew out of the need to stabilise the structure and form new spaces. The concrete forms the tectonic core of this project. Commenting on the selection of Douglas Fir to face the shuttering, Daniel Rosbottom of drdh observed that:

'Douglas fir has a high sugar content, which means that the finest particles in the concrete, which move to the outside surface during the drying process, never quite cure. When the shutters were removed the grain of the timber took the finest particles with it, leaving a clear echo of the timber planks on the concrete itself.'

The same species of timber was also used to line parts of the interior and this was dimensionally coordinated with the shuttering, resulting in a construction which combines the warmth of timber lining with the memory of that timber in the surface of the concrete, see Figure 4.34. Rosbottom noted:

'We did a series of small test casts with the contractor to explore which concrete mix to use and how long to cure it before we removed the timber shutters. We also tried a series of casts to test the colour of the concrete. Originally, we wanted to cast the armature in a whiter concrete with a lot of mica in the surface so that it glittered but we had sourcing difficulties and could not find anyone in London who would mix us the small amount that we needed. So we went for a standard mix using a 10 mm rather than 20 mm aggregate and, in retrospect, we are very pleased with the result. It is a London project so it's right that we should use London concrete, which is mixed using beach sand. It has a warm grey tone to it which works well, giving the interior a warm surface feel, so it was a good choice.'[7]

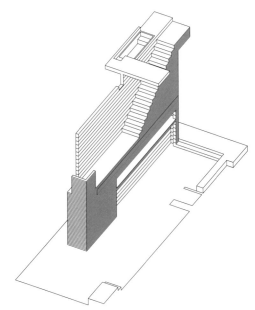

4.41 Axonometric of the basement staircase in the Kahn House, London
Designed by drdh architects

85 Swains Lane, a new build house in Highgate, London, designed by Eldridge Smerin Architects, also uses a dimensionally coordinated board marked concrete. The complete house is set out on a 99 mm vertical grid, which was generated by the stair layout and the party wall with 87 Swains Lane. The 180 mm floor zone was used for adjustment. The stair treads cantilever from the concrete walls, however, they were cast on site from the same batch of Portland cement based concrete and dowelled into position. The concrete of this house appears to be very precise, and this visual quality is achieved, in part, by the care with which the architects have detailed the internal joinery – this is either lacquered medium density fibre board or bog oak. The joinery was tailored to fit the concrete visually, suggesting precision while creating a contrast between the fine bog oak and the inherent roughness of the concrete.

4.42 The board marked concrete of
85 Swains Lane
Designed by Eldridge Smerin Architects
Engineer: Elliot Wood

4.43 Eldridge Smerin's
elevation of the interior
of the east façade,
coordinating the board
marked concrete,
including the boltholes

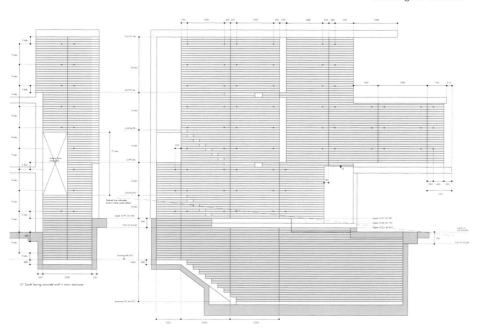

4.44 The Jones House in Randalls Town, Northern Ireland, completed 2005
Architect: Alan Jones

4.45 The OSB shuttered concrete of the Jones House

4.46 The living room of the Jones House

1. Fibre cement wall slates
2. Treated timber battens
3. Treated timber counter battens
4. Breather membrane
5. 60 mm expanded polystyrene insulation over 70 mm high-density polystyrene insulation
6. Vapour barrier
7. In situ reinforced concrete wall
8. 100 mm C35 concrete screed
9. Underfloor heating polymer pipework
10. 75 mm extruded polystyrene insulations
11. Services: water, waste, electrical ducting and gas
12. DPM
13. Precast floor unit
14. DPC
15. Dense blockwork
16. 150 mm hardcore
17. Flashed treated timber closer
18. Two layers of fibre cement wall slates as plinth facing
19. Vent
20. 20 m gravel 100 mm deep on 40–60 mm stones

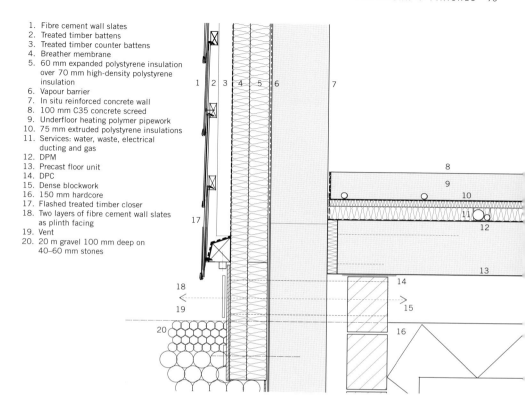

4.47 Typical perimeter plinth construction of the Jones House

The Jones House in Randalls Town, Northern Ireland, is the first project to use oriented strand board (OSB) to form the shutter face. Architect Alan Jones specifically chose to use an inexpensive OSB boarding as the formwork of the perimeter walls of his 'House of Joneses'. The selection of OSB was based on a number of factors:

- the economy of the formwork;
- its tolerance of a relatively low skilled workforce;
- its texture;
- to provide key for plaster, if necessary; and
- its originality.

He deliberately chose this board with the intention that it would leave a random, semi-natural impression on the surface of the concrete. This particular finish was desired not only for its ability to disguise any inadequacies in workmanship, but so that the building could be visually linked to the ruggedness of the surrounding landscape. Alan Jones noted that 'using orient strand board as formwork is forgiving in terms of on-site workmanship, it is low cost and leaves a natural texture that gives a visually link to the landscape beyond. Although clearly man made the stands in the orient strand board are visually analogous to the fallen leaves of autumn on a forest floor.'[8]

OSB is not very durable and therefore the formwork could not be used more than twice. It was, however, reused in the form of hoardings for onsite security during the later stages of the project. The interior of the house, which uses exposed concrete as a fabric energy storage, has a wonderful, almost velvety, texture. This is truly delightful concrete.

Polymer mould linings

The new Scottish Parliament building by Enric Miralles with RMJM, which was completed in 2004, contains a number of precast concrete elements that are highly wrought in terms of form and finish, and could not have been achieved economically without the use of digital fabrication techniques. These elements included the precast vaulted floors and internal walls, the cladding to the debating chamber, press tower and the boundary wall along Canongate.

It was the complex patterning of this final element that proved the greatest challenge.

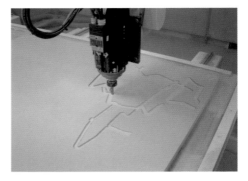

4.48 CNC machining of medium density fibreboard to form the silicone inserts of the precast concrete of the Scottish Parliament building
Designed by Enric Miralles with RMJM

Many of the elements were curved and contained inlays and contouring with individual patterns and sketches of Edinburgh by Enric Miralles. Three-dimensional computer models were produced by RMJM for each element. These were translated into machine-readable code by the mould makers, Patterns and

4.49 Silicone polymeric lining in the wooden precast mould

4.50 A precast concrete panel of the Scottish Parliament building

Moulds, who had purchased a five-axis CNC router to carry out the work. The router produced a full-size positive form of the patterning on medium density fibreboard, which became the master moulds for the cast silicone rubber mats. These were used to line the timber moulds into which the concrete was poured by the precasters Malling Products. The advantage of the silicone rubber linings was that each individual pattern template could be laid inside a standard mould for all of the boundary wall elements. By using silicone they could also achieve the curvature required from the original flat medium density fibreboard surface.

4.51 Scottish Parliament Building as viewed on Canongate, Edinburgh, in 2009

4.52 Anderson House by Jamie Fobert

For the in situ cast concrete walls of the Anderson House near Oxford Circus, London, architect Jamie Fobert selected a radically different technique. He had the timber shutters lined with cellophane, this gave the concrete surface wrinkles and visual discontinuity, creating an inexpensive, but visually rich texture. When the concrete is set, the formwork is removed and the plastic film is stripped off. This is, in essence, an experimental process and Fobert has had to demolish sections cast in a similar manor on another project when the client rejected the appearance of the concrete.

4.53 Detail of the Anderson House showing the 'wrinkled' concrete soffit

Jean Novel has subsequently used this type of wrinkly concrete on the Concrete Hall at the Headquarters of Radio Denmark in Copenhagen. A similar result can be achieved, perhaps more gently wrinkled, by casting concrete onto paper. This forms components in an installation by Frances Stacey, entitled *Never Settling Anywhere* (2009). Stacey uses common architectural materials to draw in space.

Corrugated or ribbed shuttering

Typically a ribbed surface is produced by fixing timber sections to the face of the shutter, against which the concrete will be cast. The Elephant and Rhino Pavilion at Regent's Park Zoo, London (1965 design by Casson and Conder), is a highly expressive example of ribbed concrete. The outer faces of the ribs were mechanically treated to expose the aggregate; and it has been described as marvellously expressive of its inhabitants.[9] Precast concrete moulds are often highly modelled and this is typically achieved by skilful joinery that will form the face of the

4.54 *Never Settling Anywhere* (2009)
Artist Frances Stacey – timber marquetry and cementatious castings

precast mould. CNC routing is an alternative means of achieving a similar visual quality.

Reusing formwork

In the twentieth-first century a key societal imperative is to minimise or avoid waste, and one strategy for formwork is reusable systems, as discussed above, for timber formwork its incorporation in the completed project is a desirable and project-specific option.

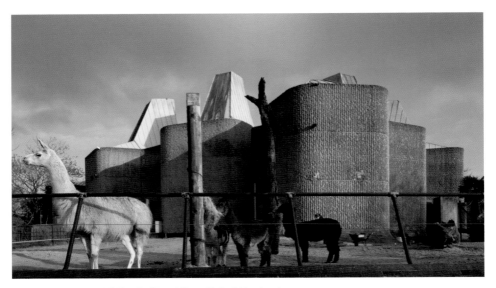

4.55 The Elephant and Rhino Pavilion at Regent's Park Zoo, London
Designed by Casson and Conder

The future use of timber formwork is often ambiguous and, in the past, has frequently resulted in it simply being burnt. To avoid this wastage, Sambuichi Architects' design for a ceramics store and studio in Hagi, Japan, reuses cedar formwork in the form of window shutters and floor planks. In the case of the floor construction, the soffit takes on the appearance of the timbers, which are directly mirrored in the timber floor below. The placing of wall formwork as window shutters adjacent to cast concrete walls has a similar effect. Depending on the exposure, the yellow-tinted cedar mellows to a silver grey to blend with the concrete. This project demonstrates a considered modularity with the virtual structure of the shuttering of the cast concrete and the elements that formed it in close juxtaposition.

4.56 Timber formwork and resultant concrete of the ceramic store and studio in Hagi

4.57 The completed interior of the ceramics store and studio, Hagi, Japan
Designed by Sambuichi Architects

4.58 Timber formwork being stored for reuse and being used to form the floor of the studio

Mechanical treatments

The cast surface of the concrete can be mechanically treated to create various effects – indeed many of these methods were originally developed by masons to texture stone. The following are the primary techniques:

- Bush hammering – the surface is worked, by hand or machine, with a bush hammer to a depth of around 6 mm.
- Comb chiselling – the surface is worked, by hand or machine, with a bolster chisel to a depth of 4–5 mm, not suitable for use with hard aggregates.
- Embossing – the surface is worked by bolster chisel or stonemason's hammer to a depth of 5–6 mm.
- Point tooling – the surface is worked with a pointed chisel to a depth of 5–10 mm.
- Grinding – the surface is ground off by 4 mm; tooling marks may show.
- Fine grinding – the surface is ground off by filing and then fine grinding, removing a total depth of around 5 mm.
- Polishing – the surface is worked to a depth of around 5 mm with fine abrasives.
- Blasting – the surface is removed to a depth of 1–2 mm by blasting the surface with sand, water and sand or steel shot.
- Flame texturing – hardened concrete is exposed to a flame at around 3,200°C, removing 4–8 mm from the surface to produce a rough finish.

See DIN V 18500:2006-12 *Cast stones* for detailed information on surface treatments.

Mechanical treatments can be used as a means of resolving problems with the visual quality of as cast concrete. Such problems were encountered with the quality of the as cast concrete structure of One Centaur Street, by dRMM Architects. This was resolved by light sand blasting, which removed the surface or laitance of the concrete (see Figure 5.1).

Chemical treatments

The surface of the concrete can also be modified by the use of a chemical reagent. Methods include the following:

- Acid etching – this exposes the aggregate by removing the surface or laitance of the cast concrete. Typically about 0.5 mm is removed by a wash of diluted acid, which is then rinsed off.
- Retardant – a surface retarder is applied to the shuttering or mould, which stops the cement setting. It is then washed, removing the unhardened cement and sand, typically to a depth of 2–6 mm. Fresh or uncured concrete can be treated in a similar way, but must be washed immediately.

Digitally delivered retardant

The external skin of the Eberswalde Library, designed by Herzog and de Meuron, incorporates a series of photographically imprinted concrete and glass panels – images from newspapers, magazines and personal photos selected in collaboration with the artist Thomas Ruff. These were applied to the concrete by transferring them onto a plastic film using the techniques of silk-screen printing, but with a cure retardant instead of ink. The idea behind the printed façade came from the technique of Sgraffito, which was used to decorate Italian Renaissance palaces and can still be seen today in old farmhouses in Alpine Switzerland. This method used a dark coloured plaster, coated with a lighter stucco, into which patterns were engraved.

The printed film is placed on the inside face of the formwork and concrete is poured over the top of it. Depending on the tonal variations of the image, different strengths of cure retardant are applied to the silk-screen, which causes the drying times of the concrete surface to vary. When the concrete sets, it is removed from the formwork. Areas of the surface that were in contact with the cure retardant remain wet. The concrete panel is washed with brushes and the unset concrete is rinsed away. This causes

4.59 The Eberswalde Library – imagery has been
etched into the surface of the concrete
Designed by Herzog and de Meuron

areas of exposed concrete to be left at varying
distances away from the true face of the panel.
The darker, rougher areas contrast with the
appearance of the fair-faced concrete, which
gives a visual appearance of a pixelated pattern.
The exact visual result cannot be predicted as
weather conditions may interfere with the curing
times of the retardants, which also means that
no two panels will be the same, unless the
process is undertaken in controlled internal
conditions.

4.60 Hepworth Museum, Wakefield
Architect: David Chipperfield

Colour

The colour of the finished concrete is controlled by both the mix and the casting method. The finest particles in the mix have the greatest effect on the surface colour. Unless a pigment is used, the finest particles in the mix are the cement, thus, the colour of cement has the greatest effect, as the finer parts of the mix tend towards the surface. To maintain a constant colour, therefore, cement must be used from the same source throughout. The colour of the sand can also play a significant role, particularly if it is very fine (known as ultra-fines), while the aggregate itself will have a significantly greater effect over the colour, if the surface is removed by post-treatment. If a consistent colour is required, the mix needs to be carefully controlled (as discussed in Chapter 2).

Colour is also influenced by the type of cement, its proportion in the mix and its curing time within the formwork – typically the longer, the darker. The characteristics of the material used to make the formwork are also influential; the key issues are the moisture absorption properties of the shutter face, discolouration from oils or release agent, or the escape of water and cement. All materials that form part of the mix should be considered and tested via a sample panel or component. For example, the use of ggbs will have a very different effect on the colour when compared with fly ash. Concrete cast against new uncoated timber boards that absorb moisture will be lighter than concrete cast against older or re-used boards, which are less absorbent.

4.61 Stained precast concrete cladding of Mustakivi School
and Community Centre, Helsinki
Designed by ARK-house arkkitehdit Oy

Pigments can also be used in the mix to modify the colour. Pigments typically have a particle size of 50 microns and thus are the finest particles in the mix significantly influencing the colour. Pigments produce subtle colours in combination with grey Portland cement, and brighter colours in combination with white cement. In order to last, they must be both UV and alkali-resistant. The Hepworth Museum, Wakefield, designed by David Chipperfield Architects was cast in situ using Portland cement based concrete to which 4% of pigment has been added. The architects described the colour as Hepworth Brown. The colour of the in situ concrete of the Hepworth appears to change from an almost steely grey to aubergine depending on the weather conditions. The pigment manufactured by Lanxess is a combination black and red pigments in the proportions 82.5 black to 17.5 red. This mix was established via samples and mock ups, a self-compacting additive was also used to minimise blowholes, the effect of the release oil on the shutter face and the anti graffiti coating were also carefully considered.

Acid stains usually consist of water, hydrochloric acid and acid-soluble metallic salts. This mixture is applied to a clean and pre-dampened concrete surface using a technique that enables a uniform distribution of the liquid, such as the use of a sprinkling can. The stain works by penetrating the surface of the concrete and reacting with the hydrated lime in the concrete mix, which consequently causes a light etching to occur on the surface of the concrete. This, in turn, allows the metallic salts to penetrate more easily, making the staining permanent. While the chemical reaction is taking place, the solution bubbles. Once the bubbling has stopped, the surface is flushed several times with water, usually containing sodium carbonate to neutralise the acid. The surface is then scrubbed to remove as much of the powdery reside from the pores as possible.

4.62 Nottingham Contemporary, which opened in 2009
Designed by Caruso St John Architects

The Nottingham Contemporary, designed by Caruso St John Architects, uses a green pigmented concrete – basically this is a white cement-based mix using Criggion fine and course aggregate to which a green oxide pigment, manufactured by W. Hawley & Sons, has been added. For the polished black precast bases, as shown in Figure 4.63, the mix is based on black quartz aggregate with white cement and a black oxide pigment. Potentially the more remarkable aspect of this cladding is the texture of Nottingham lace, which has been incorporated in the primary elevations and the tops of units on Fletcher Gate. This art gallery is located on the edge of Nottingham's Lace Market. An exemplar of Nottingham lace was three-dimensionally scanned by John Angus, Director of Textile Studies at the University of Derby, and a silicone rubber lining was produced, which Trent Concrete used to line its timber moulds before casting the panels. The green concrete is set off by golden anodised aluminium caps, which act as joint closers. Inspired by Louis Sullivan's organic yet 'high tech' facades and the nineteenth-century building of the Lace Market, Adam Caruso observes 'Modern precast is an amazing material, very fine, and we were explicitly connecting to a nineteenth century way of making a façade.'[12]

Table 4.2: Guidance on the selection of coatings for concrete

Coating type	Applications	Appearance	Surface preparation
Epoxy resins	For protection against mild corrosion and as a decorative waterproof coating for walls, floors and tanks. Ideal in maintaining breathability as it protects by penetrating the concrete. Suitable as a primer	Pigmented or clear, smooth, tough ceramic-like 2–4 mm layer, which can be cleaned easily	Excellent adhesion to damp concrete Surface must be clean and free from foreign matter by sand blasting or mechanical abrasion
Water-based epoxy resin coatings	For resistance to salt and chemical intrusion, such as in marine environments, chemical and industrial plants, power plants, food processing areas, concrete parapet walls, bridge pier caps and concrete floors	Typically standard colours of white, beige and grey Smooth and tough ceramic-like finish	Excellent adhesion to damp concrete Surface must be clean and free from foreign matter by sand blasting or mechanical abrasion
Coal tar epoxy resins	For corrosive environments, such as plants and mills, and non- visual building components, such as foundation walls and slumps	Cures to a hard smooth black-coloured surface	Light sandblasting prior to coating
Solvented coatings	For applications that require superior adhesion and durability, chemical resistance, corrosive protection, quick cure and easy cleaning Can be used as a primer where corrosion resistance or fast cure is required. Can be used as a sealer for porous surfaces, such as towelled, poured or precast concrete	Produces a ceramic-like coating	Surface must be clean and free from foreign matter by sandblasting, mechanical abrasion or acid etching
Polyurethanes	Typically used as a protective and decorative floor coating for interior and exterior applications, especially in environments which need to withstand pedestrian traffic. It is ideal for concrete floors and walls in warehouses, storage facilities, aircraft hangers, animal housing, and vehicle maintenance facilities	Additives and pigments can achieve a wide range of colours while achieving a water-resistant surface. Glossy finish	Acid etching or sandblasting prior to coating. Surfaces must be dry and free of foreign matter A fine aggregate may be incorporated into the coating to provide a slip resistant surface (floor applications)
Silicate paints	For concrete components which need to be breathable and allow water vapour to permeate Protective and decorative finish for renders subject to harsh climatic conditions. Typically used externally to prevent corrosion and commonly used for conservation schemes	Soaks into surface and therefore creates a natural, no gloss finish Typically lightfast earthen and mineral colours without toxic heavy metal pigments Can have colour variations for decorative effects	Can apply to damp (clean) concrete surfaces

Release agents

It is vitally important to all concrete that one can strike the concrete, readily remove the formwork, or remove the precast concrete from the mould. This is dependent primarily on two factors: the design of the formwork and the use of a release agent. Release agents reduce the bond between the concrete and the formwork. Commonly-used release agents are painted or pre-coated surfaces to the formwork, waxes, proprietary formulations and mineral oils. The use of release agents also has the potential to affect the finished colour. Note that wax release agents tend to create more blowholes than other types of release agent.

Coatings

Surface hardness and durability must be considered when designing in unfinished (fair-faced) concrete. Concrete is a highly resistant to surface degradation if it is constructed with careful attention to the mix, placement and curing. Coatings are rarely necessary and should not be employed to compensate for anticipated inadequacies in workmanship. However, it can be difficult to avoid efflorescence and soiling to the concrete surface if the surface is under frequent exposure to weathering. In this instance, it is possible to plan for impregnation or coatings to contribute to the reinforcement of the concrete surface. The coating used can be specified to have a subtle appearance, or it can be chosen to have a specific colour. In addition to decorative purposes, coatings can used to:

- enhance the durability and reduce corrosion in harsh climatic conditions;
- prevent staining and damage due to rain, weathering and drainage routes;
- prevent efflorescence;
- protect against damage in instances where the surface is subject to abrasive activity; and
- reduce a build up of dirt or dust around irregularities on the concrete surface.

Slurries

Slurries are cement-based mortars with additives and aggregates of a controlled size. They are commonly used as an alternative to coatings such as epoxies and polymers. They are capable of offering a flexible, durable, non-combustible and continuous waterproof layer. In this respect, they offer advantages over methods involving membranes or flashings, by simply adding a modified layer of concrete, rather than a new material and construction method. They are typically used as external coatings for wall faces, concrete blocks, prefabricated panels, tanks and swimming pools. Although the slurry protects the underlying concrete surface from weathering and staining, it may itself be subject to damage in the same way that an exposed concrete surface would be. Slurry coatings can allow concrete to breathe and, therefore, in application to walls, a vapour barrier is not required. More than one coat might be applied and the final layer may consist of a different mix in order to act as a decorative finish.

Slurry has a consistency similar to paint and can be applied as a spray or with a brush, roller or trowel, depending on the finish required. It typically has a standard grey, white and other pastel-coloured cement base. The properties of slurry are modified through the alteration of the mix proportions and by introducing new ingredients, such as plastic modified slurry, which increase the waterproofing properties and resistance to abrasion.

4.63 The base of Nottingham Contemporary is polished
black precast concrete on which the inverse order
of lace 'columns' stand

5.1 One Centaur Street
Designed by dRMM Architects

FIVE **foundations**

'Concrete is the perfect medium for house construction – it has character,
it can support itself, it is self finished and is one process.'
Alex De Rijke of dRMM Architects describing One Centaur Street, London[1]

Structure is a fundamental precursor of defined space. All architecture requires structure, resisting the force of gravity and resolving the load into the earth.[2] The typical starting point in construction on site is the foundations. To be able to design the foundations of a new building or infrastructure it is essential to establish the loads, both dead loads and live loads, that will be exerted on the foundations, and the soil properties and condition also need to be established. Both are firmly within the realm of the structural engineer, but cannot be overlooked by the architect, for they may have a very significant influence on the architecture. The conceptual starting point for the Kahn House by drdh architects, as discussed in Chapter 4, in essence began with the need to form new foundations to an existing house. This developed into the spatial arrangement providing the source or basis for the complete project.

The live loads are defined by codes of practice and the dead load is the total weight of the structure. The foundations also need to resist wind loads on the superstructure. One of the engineer's first tasks is to undertake a desktop study of the ground conditions of the site; typically this will establish the nature of the site investigations to be undertaken. This study should reveal the overall geological conditions and the likelihood of encountering buried services. In urban areas the constructional history of the site can prove vital, as the ground may be fill and/or other material from earlier uses of the site, and the soil may be contaminated. It is also important to establish the level of the groundwater table and whether the groundwater contains sulphate salts. On most projects, and definitively when information is not available, a soil investigation will be necessary.

Foundations must transmit the loads within a structure to the ground and minimise differential settlement. The extent and type of the foundation depends primarily on the loading and the ground condition. Foundations are grouped into two major classes:

- shallow foundations; and
- deep foundations.

The primary forms of shallow foundations are:

- pads;
- strip footings; and
- rafts.

The primary forms of deep foundations are:

- piles;
- contiguous piled walls;
- diaphragm walls; and
- caissons.

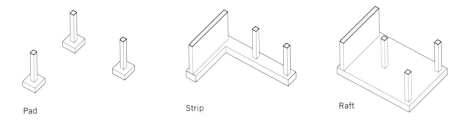

Pad   Strip   Raft

5.2 Primary forms of shallow foundations

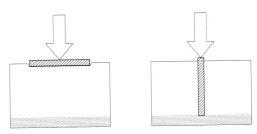

5.3 A diagrammatic comparison of raft and piled foundations: raft foundations resist loading by spreading the load, like a man spread-eagled in mud. Piled foundations resist load by either reaching bedrock or the frictional resistance of the pile in the subsoil

Table 5.1: Options for retaining walls[3]

Idealised site conditions	Idealised soil types		
	Dry sand and gravel	Saturated sand and gravel	Clay and silt
Working space available to allow ground to be battered back during wall construction	Gravity or cantilever retaining wall Precast concrete crib wall	Dewatering during construction of gravity or cantilever retaining wall	Gravity or cantilever retaining wall
Limited working space	King post wall as temporary support Contiguous piled wall Diaphragm wall	Secant bored pile wall Diaphragm wall	King post wall as temporary support Contiguous piled wall Diaphragm wall
Limited working space and special controls on ground movement	Contiguous piled wall Diaphragm wall	Secant bored pile wall Diaphragm wall	Contiguous piled wall Diaphragm wall

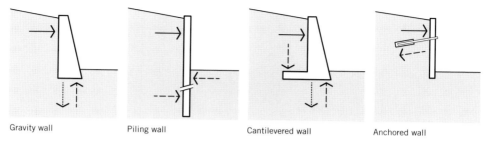

Gravity wall   Piling wall   Cantilevered wall   Anchored wall

——→ Earth pressure vector

---→ Reactive force vector

·······→ Gravity vector

5.4 Sections through generic retaining walls

There are four primary types of earth-retaining walls:

- cavity;
- piled;
- cantilever; and
- anchored.

Figure 5.4 illustrates how each of these types of retaining wall resists the pressure of the earth and resolves this load path. Another key consideration is how to deal with the groundwater that may well be present and how this is drained or whether the retaining wall needs to be tanked or constructed with a cavity to prevent water ingress.

Shallow foundations can be used if the surface soils are sufficient to resist the loading of the structure. The topsoil of a greenfield site, which has been weathered and comprises plant material, will need to be removed. Topsoil is typically 150 mm to 250 mm thick and is valuable, and so should be saved for reuse or supplied to an appropriate site. If shallow foundations are sufficient, the depth will be dependent on the soil type and the inherent risk of shrinkage. A minimum depth of 900 mm is recommended by the Building Research Establishment (BRE) on all types of clay soil.

5.5 Reinforcement cages set out to form the raft foundation of Indescon Court, E14, London (note the presence of existing piled foundations)

In non-clay soils the depth of frost-induced heave will dictate the minimum depth of the foundations. The proximity of trees will also be a consideration. A shallow foundation can be formed by increasing the depth of the ground slab, for example, to support a masonry wall. The underside of the foundation must be located below the frost line to prevent the foundation from lifting due to ice formation. Strip foundations support inline loads, such as walls or closely placed lines of columns. Reinforcement can be avoided if the strip is of sufficient size. Trench fill foundations are a variation on strip foundations where a trench is dug and this is filled with mass concrete – if the ground conditions are suitable, this can prove to be a cost-effective form of foundation.

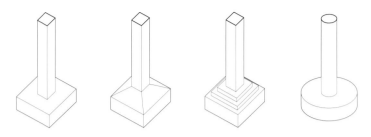

5.6   Types of pad foundations

Pad foundations support point loads, such as columns, and can be circular, square or rectangular (though circular pads require around 50% less reinforcing). Pads can be of uniform thickness or they can either be stepped or tapered to transfer greater loads. Raft foundations spread loads over a large area by means of a continuous ground slab. Rafts are practical where loads are close enough that pads would interact. The slab thickness can be increased beneath walls and columns to increase stiffness. A continuous raft foundation is also able to minimise differential settlement and is suitable for use over loose soil types.

Deep foundations are used to transfer loads to strata if surface soils are unsuitable. Piles are capable of transferring loads by means of both end-bearing and skin friction. End-bearing piles terminate in incompressible material,

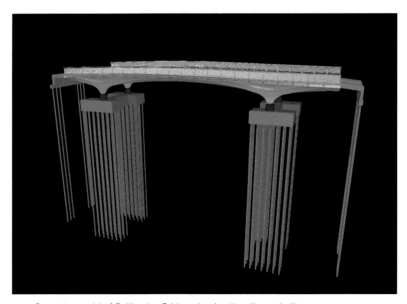

5.7   Computer model of Ballingdon Bridge, showing the piles and pile caps
Designed by Michael Stacey Architects; Engineer: Ove Arup and Partners

5.8 A flight auger piling rig

such as rock or dense gravel. Friction piles can be used where an incompressible material is unreachable; in this instance, loads are transmitted by both end-bearing and surface friction. Displacement piles (precast) are driven into the ground by means of driving, screwing, vibration or water jet. Precast piles can be produced either on site or off site, and, like circular columns, they may be spun horizontally to reduce imperfections. Bored piles (in situ) are cast into boreholes in the ground. First the borehole is augered out and the subsoil is removed, then a reinforcement cage is lowered into this shaft and finally the concrete is pumped in, surrounding the reinforcement and filling the void. The ground survey undertaken for Arup on Ballingdon Bridge showed that it was necessary to bore piles down 22 m to establish sufficient frictional resistance to the dead weight of the structure and the applied loads of articulated lorries, as defined by the Highways Agency. Furthermore, the remains of three previous bridges on the site had been revealed by archaeological examination of the site, so a bored mini-pilling rig was selected due to the need to drill through this existing archaeology.

5.9 A percussion drive piling rig: driving precast concrete piles

5.10 Precast foundations – produced by Roger Bullivant Limited

Table 5.2: Guide to the selection of Foundation[4]

Soil conditions	Suitable foundations	Comments
Rock, hard sound chalk, sand or gravel to great depth	Shallow foundations: strips, pads, rafts	Avoid the base of the foundation being below groundwater level Minimum depth to underside of foundation to avoid frost heave: 450 mm Deep foundation may be required where there are uplift conditions
Uniform firm and stiff clays to great depth, without significant trees in the vicinity	Shallow foundations: strips, pads, rafts	Minimum depth to protect against shrinkage/heave – 900 mm Trench fill can be economic
Uniform firm and stiff clays to great depth, where vegetation could impact on the shrinkage/expansion of the clay	Options: 1. Piles 2. Deep trench fill (strips) 3. Rafts 4. Piers	Refer to Table 5.4 for strip foundation depths in proximity of trees Use suspended floors with void formers
Firm clay to shallow depth over soft clay to great depth	For lightweight structures, strips, pads or rafts may be appropriate For heavy structures deep foundations will be required	For shallow foundations ensure the load is distributed over a large enough area for the soft clay to support it
Loose sand to great depth	Options: 1. Raft 2. Ground improvement with shallow foundations 3. Piles	Vibration and groundwater changes can induce settlement after construction Driven piles will increase the density of the sand
Soft clay	Options: 1. Piles 2. Wide strip foundation 3. Rafts 4. Ground improvement with shallow foundations	Strip foundations may need reinforcement Service entries into building should be flexible Rafts may not be suitable for highly shrinkable soils
Peat	Options: 1. Raft 2. Ground improvement	Suitable piles bored in situ with casing, driven in situ, driven precast Allow for drag on piles caused by peat consolidation Soils may be acidic

Soil conditions	Suitable foundations	Comments
Fill	Options: 1. Piles 2. Wide strip foundation 3. Rafts 4. Ground improvement with shallow foundations 5. Piers	Specially selected and well compacted fill will have greater load bearing capacity Service entries into building should be flexible Consider effects of contaminants in the fill
Clay, increasing in strength as depth increases (from soft to stiff clay)	Piles preferred, but a raft may be suitable for a basement	Settlement is likely to govern the pile design
Soft clay over rock at depth	Use deep foundations	Negative skin friction may add to the loads on piles
Dense sand or stiff clay over layer of soft clay, over stiff clay to great depth	Deep foundations generally required except for light loads. Ground improvement technique could be used with shallow foundations	
Mining and subsidence areas	Slip-plane raft	Piles not suitable
Sloping site	Foundations to suit soil conditions but the effects of the slope should be considered	Consider overall stability as well as local stability Groundwater will increase instability of site
Site with high groundwater lever	All foundation types may be appropriate Dewatering may be used, but consider affects on surrounding structures	In sand and gravel keep foundations above groundwater level Stability of excavations should be considered Bored piles require casing or support fluid Continuous flight auger piles suitable Ground conditions may be aggressive

5.11 The Art House, Chelsea, London – the polypropylene underfloor heating pipes are being installed above extruded polystyrene insulation prior to the pouring of the concrete ground floor slab
Designed by Brookes Stacey Randall Architects

Table 5.3: Comparison of pile types[5]

Pile type	Advantages	Disadvantages
Driven precast concrete pile	• Quality of pile can be inspected before it is placed in the ground • Construction not affected by groundwater • Can be driven in long lengths • Most appropriate in soft and unobstructed soils • No removed soil to dispose of	• Can be damaged during driving • Pile can be displaced if hits obstruction • Actual length of pile is known only when proved on site • Relatively large rig required • Noise and vibration, but piling rigs are constantly being improved • Driving force may determine pile properties • Displacement of soil may damage surrounding structures
Driven cast in situ (a tube is driven into ground and filled with in situ concrete)	• Length can be readily varied to suit actual ground conditions encountered • Can be driven in very long lengths • Driven with a closed end and therefore groundwater is excluded from hole	• Can be damaged during driving • Relatively large rig required • Noise and vibration, but piling rigs are constantly being improved • Driving force may determine pile properties • Displacement of soil may damage surrounding structures • Concrete cannot be inspected after casting • Large diameters cannot be used
Bored piles	• Can be driven in long lengths • Soil removed can be inspected • Can be installed in large diameters • End enlargements are possible in clay • Can be installed within a limited headroom • Small rigs can be used • Relatively quiet • Low vibration	• Risk of 'necking' in 'squeezing' ground conditions • Concrete is not placed under ideal conditions and cannot be inspected • Casing may be required in soils lacking cohesion • Removed soil requires disposal • May require underwater concreting • Piling rigs may be large
Augered (e.g. continuous flight auger (CFA))	• Soil removed can be inspected • The ground is continuously supported by the auger • Relatively quiet • Low vibration • Suitable for most soil types (excluding boulders) • Can be installed within a limited headroom • The continuous helical displacement technique (CHD) reduces volume of removed soil and increases soil strength adjacent to pile shaft	• Maximum 1200 mm pile diameter • Concrete cannot be inspected after pouring • Maximum pile length around 30 m • Limited length of reinforcement cage • Removed soil requires disposal • Efficiency is dependant on regular supply of concrete • Auger may be impeded by relatively stiff soils

Table 5.4: Guidance on the depth of foundations in meters adjacent to trees in shrinkable soils[6]

Species	Maximum mature height (m)	Exclusion zone 1 (m)	Exclusion zone 2 (m)
High water demand tress			
Elm, Willow	24	24.0	30.0
Eucalyptus	18	18.0	22.5
Hawthorn	10	10.0	12.5
Oak, Cypress	20	20.0	25.0
Poplar	28	28.0	35.0
Moderate water demand trees			
Acacia, Alder, Monkey puzzle, Spruce	18	9.0	13.5
Apple, Bay laurel, Plum	10	5.0	7.5
Ash	23	11.5	17.3
Beech, Cedar, Douglas fir, Larch, Pine	20	10.0	15.0
Blackthorn	8	4.0	6.0
Cherry, Pear, Yew	12	6.0	9.0
Chestnut	24	12.0	18.0
Lime, Sycamore	22	11.0	16.5
Mountain ash	11	5.5	8.3
Plane	26	13.0	19.5
Wellingtonia	30	15.0	22.5
Low water demand trees			
Birch	14	2.8	7.0
Elder	10	2.0	5.0
Fig, Hazel	8	1.6	4.0
Holly, Laburnum	12	2.4	6.0
Hornbeam	17	3.4	8.5
Magnolia, Mulberry	9	1.8	4.5

Foundation depths			
Modified Plasticity Index	Volume change potential	Outside exclusion zone 1	Outside exclusion zone 2
40% and greater	High	1.50	1.00
20% to less than 40%	Medium	1.25	0.90
10% to less than 20%	Low	1.00	0.75

Notes
1   Determine whether a particular species of tree is outside exclusion zone 1 or 2.
2   Determine the foundation depth from the lower part of the table for the particular soil conditions and the appropriate exclusion zone.
3   Where the tree(s) are inside exclusion zone 1 refer to NHBC guidelines on which this table is based.

Integration of services

Owing to its formability, concrete readily facilitates the integration of services. This has been demonstrated in earlier chapters, for example the precast components for Toyota Headquarters Building, see Figure 3.20, and it applies equally well to concrete when used to form foundations. If a project requires pile foundations, the cost of introducing into the piles, before the concrete is poured, a continuous coil of polypropylene pipe work to form the basis of a ground source heat exchange system is small and the energy saving can be very significant.

5.12 Cross section through the labyrinth of Federation Square

The Jones House in Randalls Town, Northern Ireland (see Figures 4.44–4.47) uses a horizontal loop of pipe work under the rear garden as this house did not require piled foundations. The use of a heat pump, combined with a good level of insulation, an airtight construction and exposed concrete internally, to provide thermal mass, helps to create a house with very low energy requirements.[7] Unless a ground source heat pump is powered by renewable energy, it will not achieve zero carbon as targeted by the UK for new houses by 2016 and non-residential buildings by 2019. Tony Butcher, in *Ground Source Heat Pumps*,[8] observes that a well-designed heating system for a home driven by a heat pump will require 20% to 30% of the energy required by a conventional water-based central heating system. Bill Dunster and colleagues in *The ZEDbook*[9] council against the use of heat pumps. One alternative is to construct a labyrinth of exposed concrete to preheat or precool the air, a strategy used by Wilkinson Eyre at the Alpine House, Kew Gardens in London, and on a larger scale by a consortium of architects, Lab Architecture Studio with Bates Smart, at Federation Square, Melbourne. The principle of a labyrinth is to create a large surface area of exposed thermal mass that acts as a passive heat exchanger, thus warming or cooling the incoming air. At Federation Square, 1.2 km

of interlocking concrete walls keep the atrium of Federation Square 12°C cooler than the ambient temperature, resulting in an estimated 90% saving in CO_2 when compared with a conventional air-conditioning system. Another way of constructing a labyrinth or preheating system is to bury large diameter concrete pipes through which air is drawn. This technique was used on Butterfield Park, designed by Hamilton Associates with engineers Price & Myers.

Reusing existing foundations

Some city centre sites in Europe are already congested with foundations, and instead of expensively digging out the earlier foundation an option is to reuse the existing foundation, thus saving on cost and embodied CO_2. A best practice handbook for the *Reuse of Foundations in Urban Sites*[10] has been produced, on a pan-European basis, as the major outcome of the EU-funded research RuFUS. It is presented as an authoritative technical guide and provides advice on how to address risk and guidance on decision processes for existing foundations. It also offers advice on investigation, design and construction using reused foundations. An example cited in this handbook is the new Hessian Parliament building in Wiesbaden, where, despite the new building having a

1. Min. 150 mm well compacted type 1 sub-base
2. 25 mm sand blinding
3. 225 mm RC Raft (RC30 mix 50% ggbs)
4. 5 No. T12 Lacer bars top and bottom under all load bearing walls, lapped min. 600 mm with 40 mm cover, in addition to mesh
5. A393 mesh top and bottom
6. 900 x 900 mm T12 starter bars @ 200 centres tied to mesh in wall and slab
7. 215 x 215 x 440 mm hollow concrete blocks
8. Concrete fill to hollow concrete blocks (RC30 mix 50% ggbs)
9. Bentonite-based waterproof membrane
10. Two-coat polyurethane based fully bonded liquid applied waterproof coating
11. 300 mm wide bitumen coated polyethylene strip – waterproof continuity
12. Sealing compound
13. 150 mm clear chippings for drainage
14. 200 mm extruded polystyrene insulation
15. 75 mm reinforced screed
16. Concrete fillet
17. 50 mm foil backed extruded polystyrene insulation bonded to plasterboard
18. Coir Matt

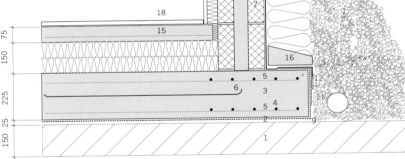

5.13 Retaining wall with external tanking to a utility
room in a house in the Lake District
Designed by Michael Stacey Architects

significantly different configuration, of the existing 81 piles, 17 were reused with 73 new piles, thus saving nearly 20% on the piling required.

Creating a dry basement

A key decision in the design of foundations and substructure may be the need to construct a dry basement. The key considerations are the use of the basement – does it need to remain totally dry (as in the basement of a library or archive), or can it be a freely ventilated space for storage (such as a cantina of a vernacular Italian Tower House)? The other key variable is the level of the water table, which may vary with the weather and seasons. There are

5.14 The London Eye
Designed by David Marks and Julia Barfield of Marks
Barfield, with initial engineering by Jane Wernick

proprietary systems for tanking the inside
or outside of a retaining concrete structure.
Guidance is provided in BS 8007:1987: *The
Code of Practice for the Design of Concrete
Structures Retaining Aqueous Liquids*. If a
fully dry basement is required, say in a library,
the only certain approach is to build a double
wall construction with a mechanically pumped
sump.

Flood risk

With climate change now established as
a significant threat to the well-being of
humankind, the need to consider flooding
in the design of the basement and ground
floors of properties within a flood risk area has
become an active design criterion. Flooding is
a risk that the Netherlands has always taken
seriously. There are three principal ways to
manage this risk:

- on an infrastructural basis with flood
  defences – such as the Thames Barrier,
  London, which was first used defensively
  in 1983;
- in the design of the architecture by raising
  the ground floor above the flood plan – see
  Hopkins Architect's design of a Green King
  draught beer cellar in Suffolk in 1980,
  where the ground floor slab is raised up
  on short concrete columns to facilitate the
  loading of beer lorries and to resist flooding
  from the River Linnet;[11]
- design the ground floor to be resilient
  during flooding.

In all cases, concrete has an important role to
play. In the last example it is possible to detail
the ground floor of, say, a home in materials
that are not damaged by flood water and that
can simply be cleaned once the flood water
has subsided. A brick and plastered wall would
be significantly damaged by flood water, the
plaster would needed to be removed and the
wall allowed to dry out, and then it would need
to be re-plastered – a process that would take
weeks, if not months, to carry out. Contrast this

5.15 Inside the reinforcement cage of the foundations
of the London Eye

with, say, a well-detailed reinforced concrete
wall, potentially faced with ceramic tiles. This
would just need to be pressure washed.

It is worth noting that the design of a project's
superstructure can have a very marked
effect on the foundation design. A dramatic
example of this is the London Eye (architects
David Marks and Julia Barfield). The moving
wheel of the Eye is cantilevered over the River
Thames. The tendency for the wheel to topple
over (an overturning moment) is resisted by
two raked steel columns and steel tension
cables, which are anchored to the ground
by substantial in situ reinforced concrete
foundations in the form of two linked pile caps
and piles. The wheel weighs over 1,800 tonnes,
with the base under the columns resisting
compression and other tension. Often concrete
has a vital, but unseen role in architecture
and infrastructure. The compression base
supporting the Eye incorporates over
180 tonnes of high-tensile steel reinforcement
within the in situ concrete.

6.1 The barcode stone-faced precast cladding being fixed to the in situ flat slab square column concrete frame of the Potterrow Development, Edinburgh
Architect: Bennetts Associates

SIX **frames**

'The free designing of the ground-plan. The pilotis carry the intermediate ceilings and rises up to the roof. The interior walls may be placed wherever required, each floor being entirely independent of the rest. There are no longer any supporting walls but only membranes of any thickness required. The result of this is absolute freedom in designing the ground-plan; that is to say, free utilization of the available means.'
Le Corbusier [1]

The emergence of concrete frame construction and the development of Modernism were inextricably linked by Le Corbusier's *Five Points of Modern Architecture*, which placed the frame's freedom of expression and organisation at the forefront of a new architecture inspired by industry. By separating the functions of structure, partitions and envelope, frame structures created a break from the classical tradition, which was bound by solid masonry enclosures dictating the plan and the expression of the façade. Replacing walls with columns instantly frees up large areas of a plan, while reducing the overall amount of material supporting the building. Today concrete frames are used widely and take on a variety of architectural expressions. This chapter introduces the benefits of concrete frames, how they work structurally, and how the design of a frame can influence wider design issues, such as aesthetic expression, environmental strategies, construction and adaptability, over a building's entire lifetime. It also aims to explain the process of sizing structural members, in order that you can reliably approximate structural sizes for your own designs, and introduces key forms of slab and beam construction.

Having decided to use a framed structure for its adaptability, freedom of expression and minimal use of material, your next question may be 'why to use concrete?' The ability

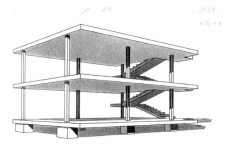

6.2 Le Corbusier's Domino House – demonstrating the architectural freedom created by a concrete frame

to expose concrete internally or externally is a major asset of the material. The potential to use a single, visually exposed material as a building's structure has long appealed to architects as a way of building 'honestly'. It can also prove economical to specify a material, such as concrete, that does not require dressing and that expresses the building's method of construction.

The principles of thermal mass and Fabric Energy Storage (FES) are described in detail in Chapter 10 on sustainability. The inherent thermal mass of concrete in an interior is a major asset, which will become increasingly important as awareness of the energy consumed by buildings grows. Slab forms, such as troughs and waffles, which increase the surface area of the soffit, can improve FES and are discussed later in this chapter.

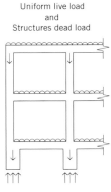

Uniform live load
and
Structures dead load

Dead and live load only

6.3 The load paths for a simple frame

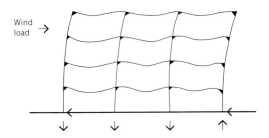

Wind load →

6.4 Deflection of a frame under wind loading is dependent on the rigid corners and the relative stiffness of the members

The inherent mass of concrete can provide acoustic separation between spaces, while the material's hard finish will affect the reflection of sound. This can be used positively in auditoria or can become problematic in spaces such as stairwells. Smooth, light finishes can improve the penetration of daylight into a building, while profiled soffits or downstand beams will create a pattern of shadows. Concrete is also fireproof, in fact it is often common to encase steel structural members in concrete in order to make them fireproof. Finally, concrete is highly suited to creating cantilevers, which can actually improve the efficiency of a structure by balancing bending moments about columns.

Figure 6.3 shows the load paths for a simple frame. In order to size structural members, one calculates the loads being supported in each member. These loads are classified as live or imposed loads, such as the weight of people, furniture and machinery, however dead loads, or the self-weight of the structure, also need to be considered. Live loads are calculated as being uniformly applied across an area of floor. The load is dependent on the building use and the following loadings are laid out in the UK National Annex to Eurocode 1: Part 1-1, 2005:

- 2.5k N/m^2 for general office loading and car parking;
- 5 kN/m^2 for high specification offices, file rooms and areas of assembly;
- 7.5 kN/m^2 for plant rooms and storage areas; and
- 10 kN/m^2 for higher specification stores.

A frame is made up of horizontal members (such as beams and slabs), vertical members (such as columns) and a means of resolving wind loading (such as cross-bracing or shear walls). The charts provided in this chapter (pages 116–147) allow you to estimate the depth of common types of floor slab. Once you know the depth of a slab, you can calculate the dead load that it will apply to any supporting beams or columns. The size of your columns is dependent on the size of all the members that they support. This means that, although the position of your columns may be the first thing that you decide on, the size of the columns will be one of the last things you can accurately calculate.

Columns

In terms of structure, columns must resist the downward forces of the slabs and/or beams that they support, as well as the bending moments from those members and from wind loading. These forces affect columns differently depending on where they are within the frame. An internal column supports loads arriving from 360° and, therefore, usually has approximately balanced bending moments and its design is governed by its compressive strength. Edge and corner columns, however, support smaller areas of floor, but are eccentrically loaded. Their design in structures up to five storeys tall is usually defined by their strength in bending. In taller structures, above seven storeys, the differences in behaviour between perimeter and internal columns are significant enough to merit different cross-sectional areas for the two types of column. Columns fail either through buckling or through crushing, depending on their slenderness ratio. Tall, thin columns

are more likely to buckle, whereas crushing occurs when shorter columns are placed under extreme loads. The high compressive strength of concrete makes failure by crushing unlikely.

The arrangement of columns within a frame influences both the layout of the space it encloses and the size of all other members within the structure. Columns are usually the most visible part of a frame and potentially the most intrusive. They are commonly laid out on grids, which describe their position. A common basis for a grid is to use multiples of 600 mm squares. Rectangular grids are often used with ratios of 1:1, 1:1.25 and 1:1.5; however, you might also consider tartan grids or non-orthogonal arrangements, such as radial, triangular or hexagonal grids. The arrangement of columns establishes the spans for horizontal members and can influence their construction. Placing columns away from the edges of your building creates cantilevers that immediately suggest a form of in situ construction. This is because of the continuity offered by in situ concrete construction and the cantilever, if it is less than a third of the span, will create a beneficial hogging moment, potentially reducing the necessary slab thickness.

Columns can be cast into square, circular, rectangular, polygonal or elliptical sections. From a structural point of view, the circular column is the most efficient, but square or rectangular columns are popular as they can simplify formwork and relate their width to that of supporting beams. Columns that are cast in situ are usually cast one storey at a time, whereas precast columns are often three or four storeys tall. The amount of reinforcement is described as a percentage, usually ranging between 1% and 4%. Increasing the amount of reinforcement strengthens the columns, but increases its cost.

As with all concrete, a column's finish is largely defined by its shuttering. Precast columns, however, can be given a smoother finish by a process known as spinning. The columns

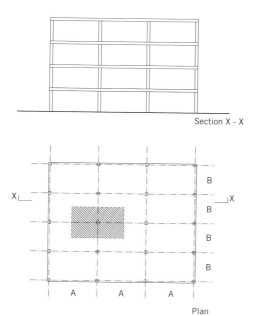

Section X - X

Plan

6.5 Area to be considered when sizing a column

are cast horizontally and then slowly rotated to prevent the formation of blowholes. Axel Schultes employed this technique in his design for the Kunstmuseum in Bonn. Peckham Library, designed by Will Alsop with engineers Adams Kara Taylor, uses columns that were cast into 323 mm diameter steel circular hollow sections to create a concrete column with an exposed surface of painted steel. Encasing steel columns in concrete is also a popular method of creating hybrid structures that blur the distinction between concrete and steel architecture. Casting concrete around steel provides fire protection to the internal member while stiffening the column.

Slabs and beams

Slabs and beams receive imposed loads, and they transfer these, along with their self-weight, into columns. The loads create a bending moment and shear forces within the beam. A beam in bending acts in compression along its lower edge and in tension along its upper edge. In a reinforced concrete beam, the concrete resists the compressive loads and the steel reinforcement resists the tensile loads. Failure to resist either of these forces will result in excessive deflection and eventual collapse. As bending moments occur about the supports, the forces are greatest towards the centre of a span. Shearing occurs where the upward force of a support counteracts the downward force on a beam. Shearing is greatest close to the ends of a beam and needs to be counteracted by the reinforcement.

6.6 The slender circular concrete columns of the excavation space of Kolumba Art Museum, Cologne, completed in 2007, are irregularly placed on the plan to avoid the gothic remains of Kolumba Church, which are now incorporated into the museum
Architect: Peter Zumthor

Applying a load to a beam causes deflection, whereby the beam physically bends and deforms. This is normally unnoticeable to the naked eye. However, deflection causes cracking, which can lead to frost damage and an eventual deterioration of the overall strength of a member. It can also appear unsightly or worrying to the untrained observer.

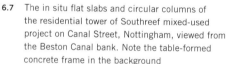

6.7 The in situ flat slabs and circular columns of the residential tower of Southreef mixed-used project on Canal Street, Nottingham, viewed from the Beston Canal bank. Note the table-formed concrete frame in the background

6.8 The in situ flat slabs, circular columns and shear walls of the residential tower of Southreef mixed-used project on Canal Street, Nottingham, with precast concrete cladding in the foreground
Architect: Levitate

Figure 6.11 shows the exaggerated deflection of beams and a portal frame under loading and the related bending moment diagram. Notice that the multiple spanning beams (D) deflect less than a single spanning beam (A). This is because, in a continuous beam, the bending on one side of a column counteracts the bending on the opposite side. Also, the two ends of the multiple spanning beam behave differently. The cantilevered end deflects less as its moment is balanced on the opposite side of the column. This means that concrete beams and slabs

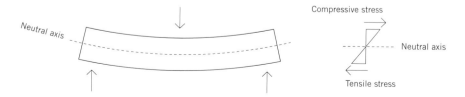

6.9 Diagram of the exaggerated deflection of a simple supported beam bending under load – showing the distribution of forces through the thickness of the beam

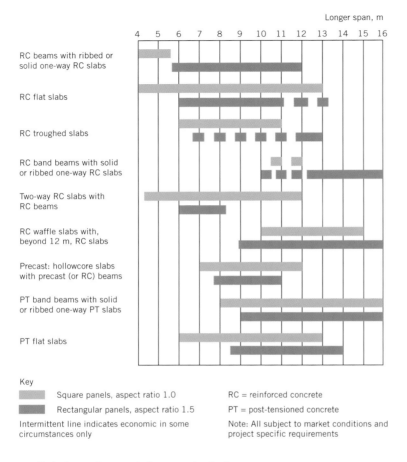

Longer span, m

| | 4 | 5 | 6 | 7 | 8 | 9 | 10 | 11 | 12 | 13 | 14 | 15 | 16 |

RC beams with ribbed or solid one-way RC slabs

RC flat slabs

RC troughed slabs

RC band beams with solid or ribbed one-way RC slabs

Two-way RC slabs with RC beams

RC waffle slabs with, beyond 12 m, RC slabs

Precast: hollowcore slabs with precast (or RC) beams

PT band beams with solid or ribbed one-way PT slabs

PT flat slabs

Key

Square panels, aspect ratio 1.0   RC = reinforced concrete

Rectangular panels, aspect ratio 1.5   PT = post-tensioned concrete

Intermittent line indicates economic in some   Note: All subject to market conditions and
circumstances only   project specific requirements

6.10 Typical spans for concrete frame construction[2]

can be thinner if they are supported away from their edges and include a cantilever. As shown in (B), if evenly loaded the ideal cantilevered is one sixth of the span.

Whether a beam is considered as single spanning or multiple spanning depends partly on whether it is precast or cast in situ. Precast systems are rarely continuous and the depths quoted in the span/depth charts represent single spans. In situ systems are largely monolithic and create multiple spans wherever

more than three columns are connected in a line. The figures quoted in the span/depth charts for in situ systems represent multiple spans, which will be thinner than spans for end spans and single spanning structures. This section includes information on generic slab types, including in situ, precast and composite systems. The merits of in situ and precast concrete are discussed in detail in Chapter 3, and they are presented together here in order that they are considered in terms of their material effects, rather than in terms of their

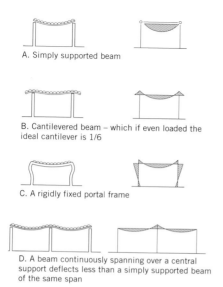

A. Simply supported beam

B. Cantilevered beam – which if even loaded the ideal cantilever is 1/6

C. A rigidly fixed portal frame

D. A beam continuously spanning over a central support deflects less than a simply supported beam of the same span

6.11 The exaggerated deflected shape and bending moment diagrams for basic structures

production. The distinction between precast and composite systems is often blurred within frames, as most precast systems need some form of on-site casting and many composite systems are based on precast assemblies with an added structural topping.

Slabs and beams can be stiffened through a process known as post-tensioning. This involves stretching steel wires placed inside the beam, which then pull against the concrete and bring the top half of the beam into compression. The effect is similar to carrying a row of books from one shelf to another by pushing in on the books at each end. Pre-stressing that is carried out on site is known as post-tensioning, while the equivalent precast process is known as pre-tensioning. Pre-stressing slabs and beams enable a longer span to be achieved at a shallower depth. The components required in post-tensioning are shown in Figures 6.13–6.16.

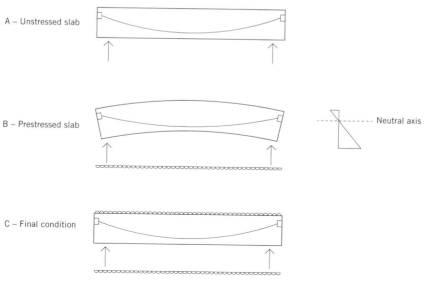

A – Unstressed slab

B – Prestressed slab

Neutral axis

C – Final condition

6.12 Diagram showing the benefit of prestressing a concrete beam

Aside from its structural role, the design of the slab is arguably the area of frame design that offers most freedom and opportunities to exploit the visual, thermal and spatial qualities of concrete construction. This section also includes information on a number of basic types of slab, including generic forms, typical spans and methods of construction. The visual appearance of a soffit can have a great impact on a space, whether it is the distinctive pattern of a waffle slab, the simplicity of a flat slab or the rugged industrial aesthetic of an exposed block and beam ceiling. Exposing a soffit can define an aesthetic as well as opening up the possibility of exploiting concrete's thermal mass. You may wish to increase the surface area of an exposed soffit and to express its method of construction or create an entirely flat slab to aid daylighting.

Horizontal and vertical services must also be considered in tandem with the structure. If you decide to expose a structure internally, this will often lead to exposing service runs, such as plumbing, wiring and light fittings, unless they are carefully integrated into the concrete. Horizontal services may have to negotiate downstand beams and ribs, while vertical

6.13 Plan view of cast-iron post-tensioning live end in the in situ concrete edge beam, Canal Street, Nottingham – plan view, before the cables have been installed

6.14 Cast-iron post-tensioning live end in the in situ concrete edge beam

6.15 Post-tensioning cables being installed before the concrete is poured

6.16 The ends of the post-tensioning cables need to be accessible during the tensioning process

facing page
6.17 In the Informatics Forum of Edinburgh University, the concrete frame, shear wall and soffits are all exposed to provide thermal mass. The soffits are painted bright colours, inspired by Eduardo Paolozzi's Turing prints
Architect: Bennetts Associates

6.18 In situ concrete core of the extension of the
BBC Headquarters on Portland Place, London
Designed by MJP Architects

services may have to pass through the floor
slab. Lloyd's of London, designed by Richard
Rogers and Partners with engineers Arup,
features a 440 mm service void between an
open grid of structural concrete beams and a
100 mm slab that provides acoustic separation
between floors. This arrangement allows
different types of services to be maintained
and replaced as time and logic dictate, see
page 151. By contrast, Sheppard Robson's
design for the Toyota Headquarters in Surrey
closely integrates bespoke precast coffers with

the provision for lighting and ventilation, see Figure 3.20. By designing service voids into the coffers at an early stage, they were able to recess ventilation intakes into the panel and create a bespoke lighting raft that reflects light off the soffit.

Well-detailed and carefully constructed concrete structures can last for hundreds of years. In this time the use of the structure will inevitably change, so a good slab system is able to adapt to new programmes and services. The ability to subdivide a concrete floor plate or cut new holes into a concrete slab is important therefore to the long-term adaptability of a structure. Your choice of slab will affect the long-term adaptability of your building. Flat slabs, for instance, can be compromised if a hole is introduced close to a column. Pre-stressed structures can also be compromised if the tensioning strands are subsequently exposed. Lloyd's of London avoids such problems by locating elements such as toilets and staircases, which are seen as ephemeral, beyond the open-plan floor plate. Many precast slabs systems, such as block and beam, are simpler to adapt, as individual elements can be removed to create a hole.

By using a frame you are immediately reducing the amount of material used in your structure. However, you may wish to reduce this further by employing a particular slab form or by including void formers within a slab's depth. Trough and waffle slabs use less concrete span for span compared with a flat slab, but they require more time, energy and materials to be used in their formwork. Lattice girder soffit slabs can include polystyrene blocks or inflated plastic balls, which decrease the weight and the amount of concrete within the slab.

Bracing and shear walls

As well as resisting forces within the structure, frames must also resist forces from the outside environment. In high winds, multi-storey frames act as vertical cantilevers. As such they require some method of transferring horizontal wind loads vertically into the ground. This is typically achieved through one of four strategies: namely, through the use of shear walls or structural cores, steel cross-bracing, concrete cross-bracing, or stiff joints between vertical and horizontal members. The location of shear walls and cross-bracing is explained in Chapter 7 on walls. These strategies minimise the cross-sectional areas of columns, but they can interfere with functional planning. Using stiff connections between members requires stronger and, therefore, larger columns, but creates uninterrupted open-plan floors.

When designing a concrete frame, you should consider the following:

- the exposure of the frame, internally and externally;
- the environmental role of the frame, including thermal, acoustic and lighting strategies;
- the use of in situ, precast or composite construction;
- the use of cantilevers;
- the building's use and imposed loads;
- the ability to cut holes through floors in the future;
- the accommodation of vertical and horizontal building services;
- the embodied energy associated with the materials and formwork;
- the ease of construction and reuse of formwork;
- the demolition of the building at the end of its useful life, and the recycling of the components or the concrete and rebar; and
- resistance to fire.

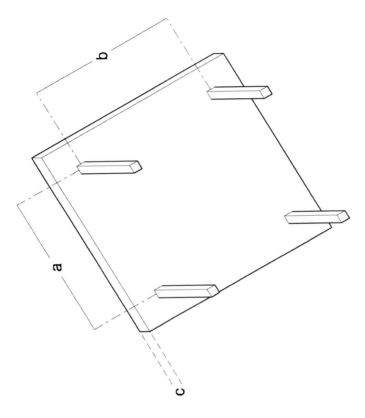

a = 4,000–12,000 mm
    6,000–14,000 mm when post-tensioned
b = 4,000–12,000 mm
    6,000–14,000 mm when post-tensioned
c > 200 mm

flat slab

Flat slabs, also known as solid slabs, offer a shallow overall thicknesses and a crisp and simple aesthetic. Simple formwork makes them quick and, therefore, cheap to build. The flush soffit makes it easy to accommodate horizontal ducts and services, and can aid natural daylighting. Partitions can be placed practically anywhere beneath a flat slab. Shearing action around the edges and around columns can be a problem, which is commonly dealt with through the use of mushroom column heads, drop panels or steel shearheads inserted in the slab. Introducing holes can be problematic. Post-tensioning can greatly increase possible spans and small units (up to 3.5 m by 4 m) can be precast for use in repetitive building types, such as hotels, student accommodation and military barracks. Flat slabs, however, have a limited surface area in terms of providing exposed thermal mass.

Key advantages

- Simple and fast formwork.
- Flexible plan for partitions and services.
- The level soffit can aid daylight.
- Readily pre-stressed for long spans.

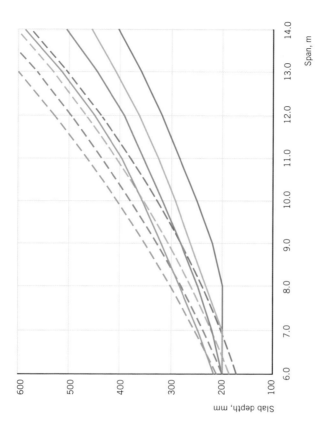

Span, m

Slab depth, mm

Characteristic
imposed load (IL)

2.5 kN/m^2
5.0 kN/m^2
7.5 kN/m^2
10.0 kN/m^2

RC slab
(Multiple spans)

Post-tensioned RC slab
(Multiple spans)

New Street Square Offices

In 2006 the frame of the New Street Square
Offices, designed by Bennetts Associates
with engineers Pell Frischmann, used post-
tensioned flat slabs to maximise the letable
area, combining relatively thin slabs with a
generous column grid. The slab thickness is
325 mm and future flexibility has been built
in by providing 'soft spots' within the slab for
openings to be formed with relative ease.
The columns are set out on a 9,000 mm x
12,000 mm grid.

flat slab with column heads

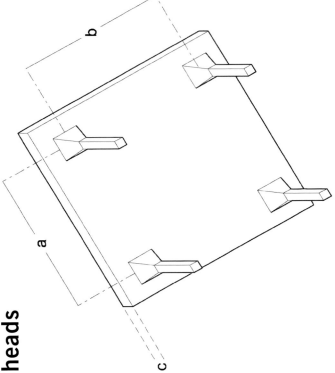

a = 4,000–12,000 mm
b = 4,000–12,000 mm
c > 200 mm

Shearing action around columns can be a problem with flat slabs, especially those with higher loadings. Introducing column heads can alleviate such problems, while reducing the thickness of the rest of the slab and retaining the simplicity of the soffit. This technique is particularly cost effective in buildings with spans from 5 m to 10 m and high loadings. As with regular flat slabs, long-term deflection can be an issue, leading to cracking around the edges where the slab meets applied finishes, such as plastered walls. Flat slabs with column heads can facilitate natural daylight and can readily accommodate services. The installation of internal partitions is straightforward except on the column grid. Column heads can also go some way to increase the surface area of the structure.

Key advantages

- Flexible plan for partitions and services.
- The level soffit can aid daylight.
- Supports higher loads.
- Pre-stress for greater spans.

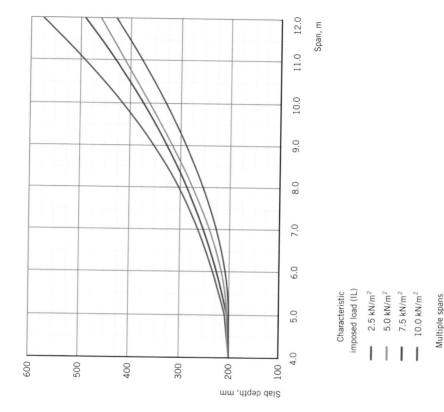

Characteristic
imposed load (IL)

— 2.5 kN/m²
— 5.0 kN/m²
— 7.5 kN/m²
— 10.0 kN/m²

Multiple spans

Slab depth, mm

Span, m

Boots Factory D10

Designed by Owen Williams for wet processes, Boots Factory D10 is described by Nikolaus Pevsner as 'a milestone in modern architecture – and especially concrete architecture',[3] he cites Rayner Banham's observation that D10 was one of the most influential modern buildings in Britain.[4] Mushroom head concrete columns support the concrete slab, as shown in Figure 6.19, surrounding the packing hall. The front façade is cantilevered out over the loading bay by 9.15 m. Boots Factory D10 combines an effective functional layout with constructional elegance. It was built between 1930 and 1932, and is still in production.[5]

6.19 Mushroom column heads of Boots Factory D10, completed in 1932

Designed by Owen Williams

one-way flat slab with beams

A one-way flat slab with beams is a very direct form of construction. Unlike a typical flat slab, this type only spans in one direction. The beams normally support the larger span and resolve the shearing problems associated with flat slabs. The slab and beams act monolithically so that the beams can be considered as T-shaped or an inverted L, depending on their location. As this system is simple to employ, it can prove quick and economical to build. Upstand beams can be used around the perimeter to improve the incidence of daylight onto the soffit. An upstand would typically be slightly deeper, but can be absorbed into the wall construction. Limited surface area makes it hard to exploit thermal mass, and downstand beams can create a problem with ceiling level service runs and can cast shadows across the soffit.

Key advantages
- Simple structure.
- Quick and simple formwork.
- Flexible plan for partitions and services.
- Readily pre-stressed for long spans.

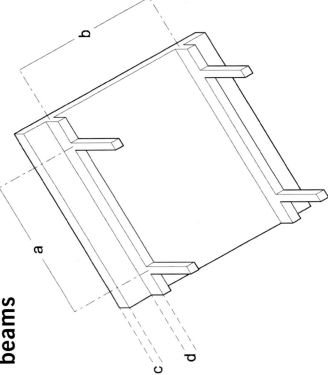

a = 4,000–12,000 mm
b = 4,000–12,000 mm
c > 150 mm when post-tensioned > 200 mm
d > 230 mm when post-tensioned > 280 mm

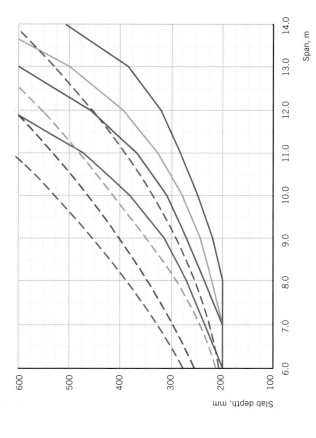

Slab depth, mm

Span, m

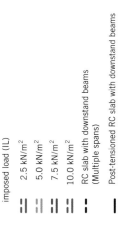

Characteristic
imposed load (IL)

2.5 kN/m^2

5.0 kN/m^2

7.5 kN/m^2

10.0 kN/m^2

RC slab with downstand beams
(Multiple spans)

Post-tensioned RC slab with downstand beams
(Multiple spans)

Slab depths can be approximated with the graph opposite. Beam depths, which are considered as including the depth of the slab, depend on the area of slab that is to be supported. Spacing beams closer together reduces their depth and the spanning distance of the slab. Beam widths are usually the same as the column width, in order to simplify formwork. The graph opposite includes the benefits of post-tensioning the slab with a marked reduction in slab depth.

one-way slab with band beams

Using wide beams with a flat slab can prove more economical than beams based on a column size for structures with light loadings. Band beams reduce the effective span of the slab, thereby reducing its overall thickness. A typical width for the band beam is 2,400 mm and it typically sits 150 mm below the soffit. The spans quoted, however, are still measured from column centre lines. Band beams and the slab are formed with reusable, demountable table form shuttering. The smaller downstand eases service routes and improves the penetration of daylight into the building.

Key advantages

- Fast, simple construction.
- Thin slabs.
- Good daylight, depending on the orientation.

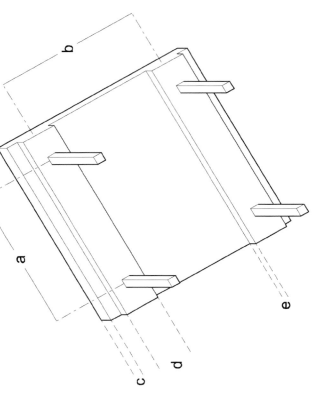

a = 4,000–15,000 mm
b = 4,000–12,000 mm
c > 150 mm when post-tensioned > 200 mm
d = typically 2,400 mm
e = typically 150 mm

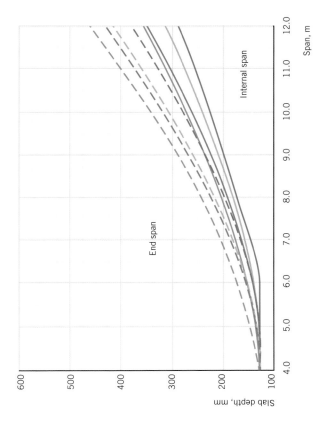

Slab depth, mm

Span, m

End span

Internal span

Characteristic
imposed load (IL)

2.5 kN/m²
5.0 kN/m²
7.5 kN/m²
10.0 kN/m²

End span
(of multiple span)

Internal span
(of multiple span)

two-way slab with beams

A two-way flat slab with downstand beams spans in two directions and, therefore, is usually used with a square grid. It is commonly used for buildings such as warehouses, where there is a high loading and relatively little servicing. The downstand beams can cause problems locating service routes, as ducts and pipe-work cannot pass through the beams. This can have a knock-on effect and increase the floor to ceiling heights and, thus, the height of the overall structure. For ease of construction, the width of the beam is typically governed by the width of the columns.

Key advantages

- Suitable for higher loadings.
- Requires regular grid.
- Readily pre-stressed for long spans.

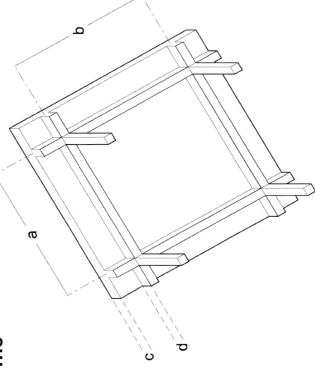

a = 4,000–12,000 mm
b = 4,000–12,000 mm
c > 150 mm when post-tensioned > 200 mm
d > 225 mm

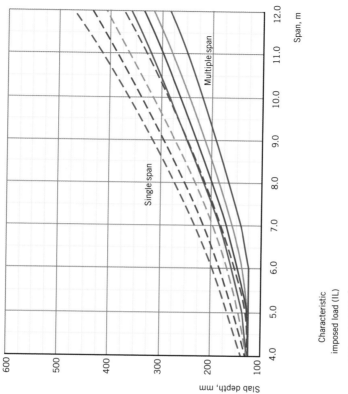

Span, m

Slab depth, mm

Single span

Multiple span

Characteristic
imposed load (IL)

- - 2.5 kN/m^2
- - 5.0 kN/m^2
- - 7.5 kN/m^2
- - 10.0 kN/m^2
- Single span
— Multiple span

ribbed slab with beams

This in situ slab introduces long recesses into the soffit to create ribs and reduce self-weight. Reducing the overall amount of concrete within the slab, while increasing the surface area, compared with a flat slab over a similar span. Ribbed slabs also have a slightly greater overall depth. The ribs span in one direction between downstand beams, although wide beams and integral wide beams are also common. Beams span the greater distance and the ribs span the shorter. The high surface area of the ribs makes this system suitable for use as part of an FES strategy. Small and large holes can be introduced into the slab. Internal partitions may require special attention if they do not run parallel to the ribs. The use of downstands can complicate service routes and special attention must be paid when locating partitions in directions not parallel with the ribs.

Key advantages

*   High surface area.
*   Easy to introduce holes.
*   Distinctive profiled soffit.
*   Voids reduce the self-weight.

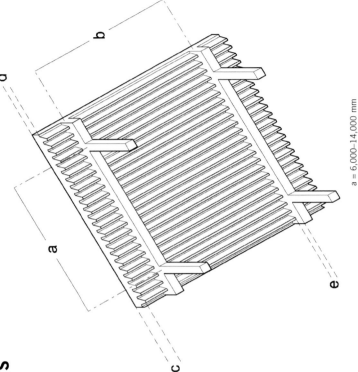

a = 6,000–14,000 mm
b = 6,000–14,000 mm
c > 250 mm
d = 100 mm
e > 100 mm

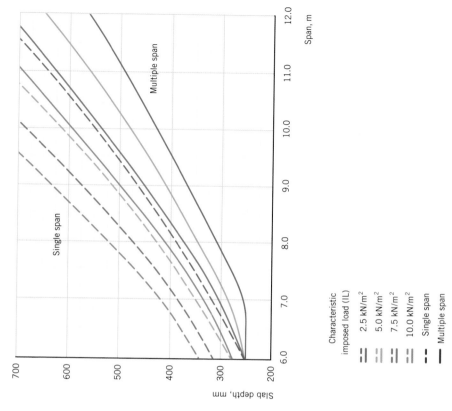

Slab depth, mm

Span, m

Single span

Multiple span

Multiple span

Characteristic
imposed load (IL)

2.5 kN/m^2

5.0 kN/m^2

7.5 kN/m^2

10.0 kN/m^2

Single span

Multiple span

The ribs are cast on site into polymer moulds, such as expanded polystyrene. The moulds are propped during casting then lowered away to be cleaned and reused. Rib profiles are adaptable, but they must be at least 125 mm thick at their base to leave room for reinforcement.

trough slab

The trough slab is similar in many ways to the ribbed slab, except that the trough slab has integral band beams, flush with the bottom of the ribs. The beams tend to be wide and heavily reinforced to counter deflection. Like the ribbed slab, the trough slab has a high surface area and can be used as part of an FES system. Maintaining a level soffit can simplify service routes and, to a certain extent, aid daylight.

Key advantages

* High surface area.
* Easy to introduce holes.
* Distinctive profiled soffit.
* Voids reduce the self-weight.

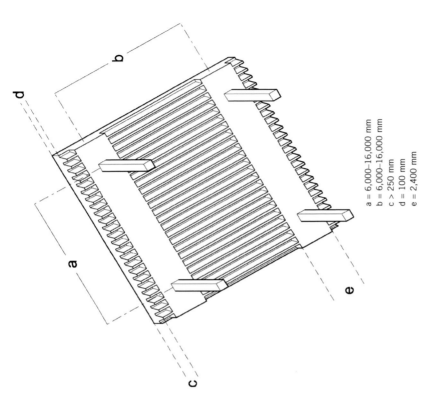

a = 6,000–16,000 mm
b = 6,000–16,000 mm
c > 250 mm
d = 100 mm
e = 2,400 mm

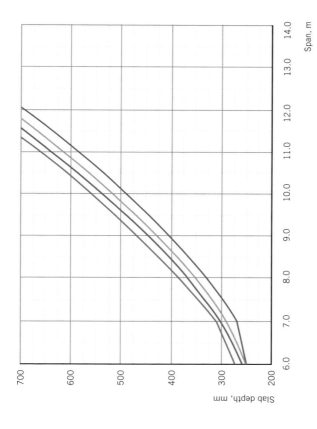

Slab depth, mm

Span, m

Characteristic
imposed load (IL)

— 2.5 kN/m^2
— 5.0 kN/m^2
— 7.5 kN/m^2
— 10.0 kN/m^2

Multiple spans

This is an in situ system, which commonly uses custom-made formwork from polystyrene or other polymers. The high-embodied energy of the formwork and its cost can be reduced by reusing the formwork. Ribs must be at least 125 mm wide at the base to allow room for reinforcement.

ribbed slab with band beams

A ribbed slab with band beams differs from a trough slab in that the wide beams stand down from the rest of the soffit, which are typically 2,400 mm wide. The extra depth can create longer spans. As with trough slabs, the ribbed slab with band beams has a high surface area and can be incorporated into an FES strategy. Holes can be introduced into the slab, but not necessarily through the beams. Detailing of the internal partitions needs careful consideration and the small downstand may complicate horizontal services.

Key advantages

- High surface area (FSE).
- Easy to introduce holes.
- Distinctive profiled soffit.
- Voids reduce the self-weight.

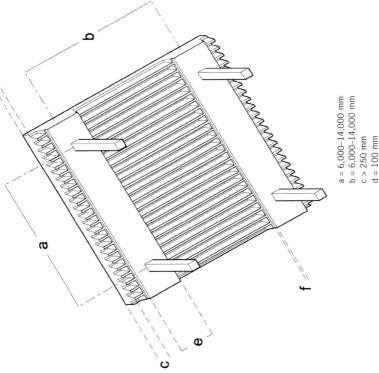

a = 6,000–14,000 mm
b = 6,000–14,000 mm
c > 250 mm
d = 100 mm
e = 2,400 mm
f = flush to 150 mm

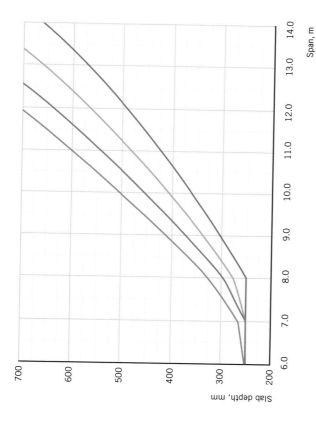

Characteristic
imposed load (IL)

— 2.5 kN/m^2
— 5.0 kN/m^2
— 7.5 kN/m^2
— 10.0 kN/m^2

Multiple spans

Span, m

Slab depth, mm

This type of slab is cast in situ. Custom profile moulds are commonly reused throughout a building's structure. The moulds are propped from below as the slab is cast. Ribs must taper slightly to ease the removal of the moulds and measure at least 125 mm at their base to accommodate reinforcement.

waffle slab

Waffle slabs have regular voids sunk into the soffit and span in two directions.

Compared with a flat slab, waffles use less concrete and have a higher surface area at the expense of deeper slabs, higher formwork costs and longer construction times. The soffit can be expressed internally and its high surface area makes it suitable for use in FES systems. The soffit creates a distinctive pattern of shadows and its appearance can vary with well-considered lighting. The location of partitions is adaptable as the ribs run in two directions. Panels around columns are usually filled in to deal with punching shears.

Key advantages

- High surface area (FES).
- Relatively easy to introduce holes for services.
- Distinctive profiled soffit.
- Voids reduce the self-weight.

The slab profile is formed by polypropylene, glass-fibre reinforced plastic (GRP) or expanded polystyrene formwork, which requires fixing on site.

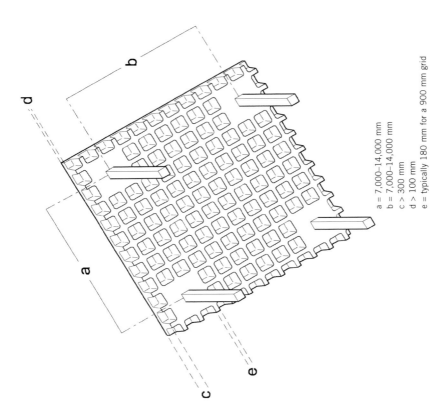

a = 7,000–14,000 mm
b = 7,000–14,000 mm
c > 300 mm
d > 100 mm
e = typically 180 mm for a 900 mm grid

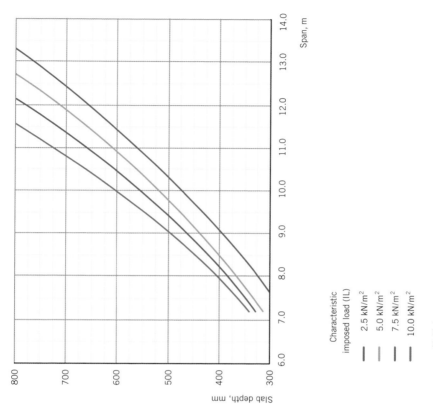

Slab depth, mm

Span, m

Characteristic
imposed load (IL)

2.5 kN/m^2
5.0 kN/m^2
7.5 kN/m^2
10.0 kN/m^2

Multiple spans

Standard moulds are square in plan and measure 225 mm, 325 mm or 425 mm deep in section, with ribs 125 mm thick at 900 mm centres. The ribs may be wider on longer spans to accommodate added reinforcement. Bespoke moulds are widely used to suit particular projects and can employ diamond or triangular grids.

National Theatre

Denys Lasdun's National Theatre in London employed bespoke GRP moulds sized to create a 1,100 mm orthogonal grid for the in situ concrete waffle slab.

precast hollow-core slab

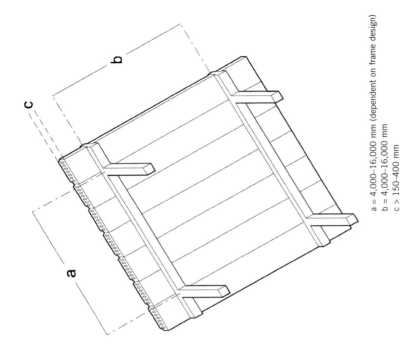

a = 4,000–16,000 mm (dependent on frame design)
b = 4,000–16,000 mm
c > 150–400 mm

Precast hollow-core slabs are the most popular form of precast construction and come in a range of sizes by different manufacturers. Essentially they are wide concrete planks, with continuous voids cast along their length. The voids reduce the self-weight of the slab. The planks are cast in steel moulds under factory conditions. Once delivered to site they are craned into position and given a levelling screed. A structural topping can be added for greater spans or higher loadings. The use of steel moulds gives a smooth finish to the soffit, which can be exposed or painted. The edges of planks have a small chamfer, which creates a bird's mouth joint between the elements on the soffit. Slab depths vary from 150 mm to 450 mm plus any screed or topping, and slab elements are typically 600 mm or 1,200 mm wide. The precast planks span between beams or walls, which may be precast or in situ. Precast hollow-core slabs can form the basis of an active fabric energy storage system (FES).

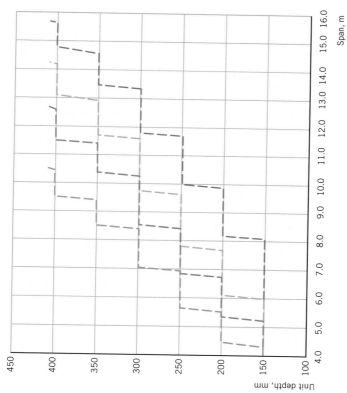

Span, m

Unit depth, mm

Characteristic
imposed load (IL)
— 2.5 kN/m²
— 5.0 kN/m²
— 7.5 kN/m²
— 10.0 kN/m²

Single span unpropped

Key advantages

- Range of spans and loadings.
- Precasting reduces time on site.
- Immediately safe working platform.
- The soffit can be exposed or simply treated.
- No propping or formwork on site.
- Can be part of an active FES system.

Elizabeth Fry Building

Some manufacturers, such as Termodeck™, use the internal voids as part of an active FES system. The Elizabeth Fry Building, by John Miller and Partners, exploits the heat exchange capacity of the voids by channelling air through the planks as part of a night-time cooling strategy. The soffit is exposed internally to absorb heat from the occupants. This is then purged from the building via a computer-controlled building management system. Incorporating ductwork into the slab also eliminates exposed ductwork and the need for a suspended ceiling.

composite hollow-core slab

To enhance their spanning capacity, precast hollow core slabs can be used as permanent formwork with reinforced concrete cast on site to create a hybrid floor structure. The hollow-core slabs are cast into steel moulds under factory conditions. These elements are then transported to site and craned into position where they provide the soffit to the floor. A typical topping is 50 mm of lightly reinforced in situ concrete. The final structure combines the factory finish of a precast element with the robust nature of in situ construction.

Key advantages

- The soffit can be exposed or simply treated.
- No propping or formwork on site.
- The soffit is produced under factory conditions.
- Flexible plan for partitions and services.
- Level soffit can aid daylight.
- Can be part of an active FES system.

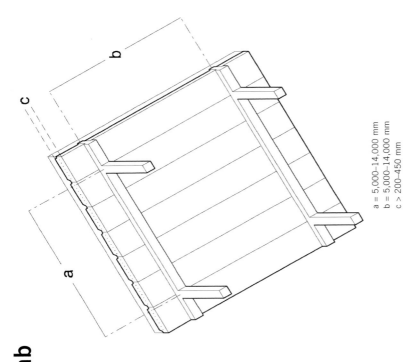

a = 5,000–14,000 mm
b = 5,000–14,000 mm
c > 200–450 mm

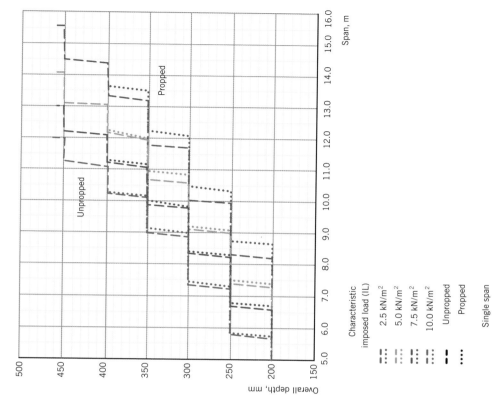

Hollow-core planks typically have small chamfers cast into the long edges of the panels, which create a bird's mouth effect in the soffit where two slabs are placed side by side. The soffits are commonly exposed in industrial environments or treated with paint, plaster or suspended ceilings in other locations. The flat soffit can aid daylight penetration and can be used as part of an active FES.

composite lattice girder soffit slab

This system uses a thin precast soffit as permanent formwork to create a hybrid flooring system. Precast into the soffit slabs are lattice beams of steel reinforcement. The soffits are craned into position, then have in situ concrete poured over them on site to create a hybrid structure. The reinforcements provide a physical connection between the soffit and the in situ topping, and lend the units rigidity during transport. The self-weight can be reduced by placing polystyrene void formers or inflated plastic balls between the girders. This system combines a factory-controlled finish and reinforcement detailing, while simplifying the transport of components.

Key advantages

- The soffit can be exposed or simply treated.
- Reinforcement and finish produced under factory conditions.
- Void formers can reduce the self-weight.
- Flexible plan for partitions and services.
- The level soffit can aid daylight.

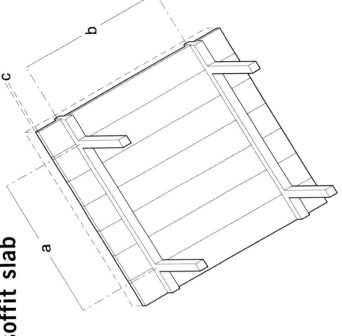

a = 3,000–9,000 mm
b = 3,000–9,000 mm
c > 115 mm

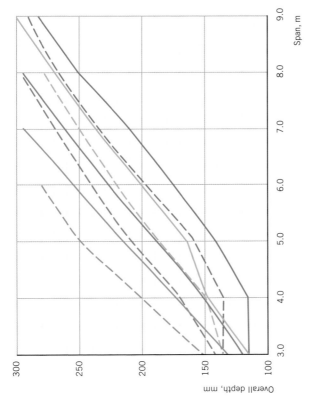

Overall depth, mm

300

250

200

150

100

3.0   4.0   5.0   6.0   7.0   8.0   9.0

Span, m

Characteristic
imposed load (IL)

2.5 kN/m^2

5.0 kN/m^2

7.5 kN/m^2

10.0 kN/m^2

Single span

Two span

Lattice girder soffit precast slabs are cast into steel moulds under factory conditions and can be left exposed or given simple surface treatments. Slab units are typically 1,200 mm or 2,400 mm wide and between 50 mm and 100 mm thick before the topping is added. The precast elements usually require propping while the in situ concrete cures. The photograph below shows a composite lattice girder slab being craned into position at More London, architect Foster and Partners.

precast beam and block

Beam and block systems are made up of inverted precast T-beams placed at close centres and filled in with either standard concrete blocks or concrete pots containing voids to reduce the self-weight. The slab is then finished with a screed. The soffit is not normally exposed, a rare exception being Piers Gough's design for Janet Street Porter's house in London.

Key advantages

- Easy to introduce holes.
- Voids can be introduced to reduce the self-weight.
- Uses small repetitive components.
- Immediately safe platform.

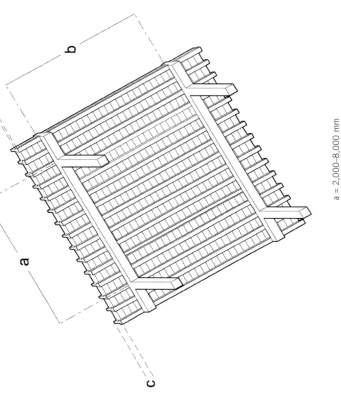

a = 2,000–8,000 mm
b = 2,000–8,000 mm
c = 150–225 mm
d > 50 mm

Characteristic imposed load (IL)

- - - 1.0 kN/m²
- - - 2.5 kN/m²
- - - 5.0 kN/m²
- - - 7.5 kN/m²
- - - 10.0 kN/m²

Single span unpropped

Janet Street Porter's House

The individual blocks are laid by hand. Once laid, drilling through the blocks or leaving the blocks out entirely can create holes in the slab for services. The typical slab thickness for domestic construction is 200 mm, excluding the thickness of the screed.

precast double tees

Precast pre-stressed double tee beams are used for long spans with high loadings, yet are relatively lightweight. They are cast under factory conditions, then pre-tensioned to increase their span capacity. Once transported to site, they are craned into position, typically comprising components 2,400 mm, 2,000 mm or 900 mm wide; tapered and non-standard sizes can be produced to suit a specific structural grid. They can be left exposed and will typically provide two hours' fire resistance. Pre-stressed double tee beams create relatively lightweight floors for large spans and have a large surface area available for heat exchange in a FES strategy.

Key advantages

- Pre-stressed and produced under factory conditions.
- Supports higher loads.
- Suitable for long spans.
- High surface area.
- Distinctive profiled soffit.

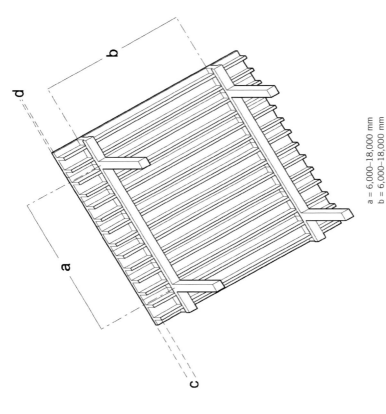

a = 6,000–18,000 mm
b = 6,000–18,000 mm
c > 300 mm
d = 50 mm

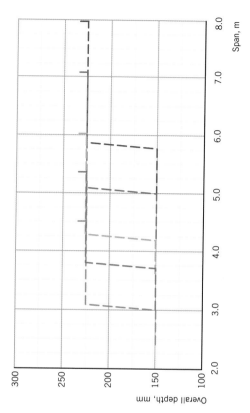

Span, m

Overall depth, mm

Characteristic
imposed load (IL)

- 1.0 kN/m²
- 2.5 kN/m²
- 5.0 kN/m²
- 7.5 kN/m²
- 10.0 kN/m²

Single span unpropped

precast double tees with topping

Precast pre-stressed double tee beams are used for long spans with high loadings. An in situ structural topping adds capacity robustness and buildability, which is typically 75 mm mesh reinforced concrete. Pre-stressed double tee beams create relatively lightweight floors for large spans. High-quality surface finishes are achievable and the soffit is often exposed, providing a large surface area that is a useful FES strategy. Once transported to site they are craned into position, typically comprising components 2,400 mm, 2,000 mm or 900 mm wide; tapered and non-standard sizes can be produced to suit a specific structural grid. The slab depth typically ranges between 375 mm and 875 mm (see graph below). Propping may be necessary until the topping has hardened. The depth of the voids within the beams can be used to carry services in one direction, but locating partitions or carrying services at right angles to the ribs can be problematic. Compared with an in situ ribbed slab, double tee planks can be erected on site more quickly and can provide a safe working platform immediately.

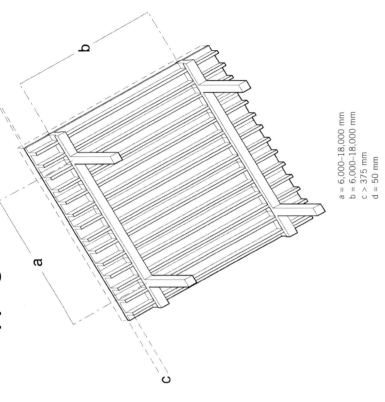

a = 6,000–18,000 mm
b = 6,000–18,000 mm
c > 375 mm
d = 50 mm

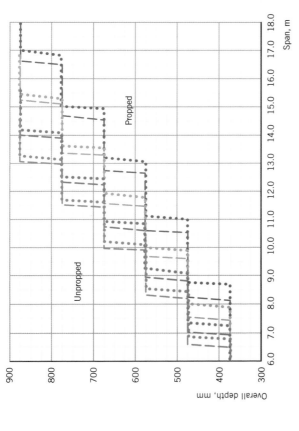

Span, m

Overall depth, mm

Unpropped

Propped

Characteristic
imposed load (IL)

2.5 kN/m^2
5.0 kN/m^2
7.5 kN/m^2
10.0 kN/m^2

Unpropped
Propped

Single span

Key advantages

- Suitable for long spans.
- Supports high loads.
- Pre-stressed and produced under factory conditions.
- Distinctive profiled soffit.
- High surface area for FES.

For further information on concrete frames, including the sizing of beams and columns, see *Economic Concrete Elements to Eurocode 2*.[6]

From the generic to the project specific

The next section on concrete frames moves from the generic to the project specific, taking three key exemplars to illustrate the potential of concrete to form architecture of the highest quality. A key question in the detailing of architecture is the development of generic options based on first principles to the project-specific detail. Often project details are imbued with cultural and economic influences that are specific to the particular project. The reuse of a detail needs to be carefully thought through and integrated into the architectural intention of a new project.

Johnson Wax Administration Building

Inspired by the natural form of forests and trees, Frank Lloyd Wright designed a bespoke structural system for the Johnson Wax Administration Building in Racine, Wisconsin. The building's main space, the Great Workroom, is dominated by an ordered forest of 'dendriform' or tree-like concrete columns. The slender tapered columns are just 230 mm wide at their base and sit on steel footings, which are practically unable to withstand bending. Wright borrowed expressions from botany to describe the three parts of the columns: the stem, the calyx and the petal. Atop the petal sits a slab, connecting columns and providing stiffness; the frame works like a table, which has stiff connections between the tabletop and

6.20 The Great Workroom of the Johnson Wax Administration Building, completed in 1939
Architect: Frank Lloyd Wright

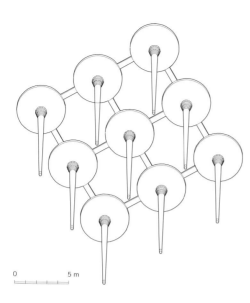

Column dimensions
230 mm diameter, tapering 2.5 degrees from the vertical

Column type
In situ concrete

Grid
6,000 mm x 6,000 mm

Number of storeys
1 (in Great Workroom)

Floor loading
Self-weight and 36 m² of roof per column

Resolution of wind loading
Stiff joints at the top of the columns

6.21 Structural arrangement of the Great Workroom of the Johnson Wax Administration Building

0   5 m

6.22 Frank Lloyd Wright witnessing the load testing of a prototype concrete column for the Johnson Wax Administration Building

the legs, but no connection in bending to the floor. Many of the columns are hollow, the outer edge measuring less than 90 mm in thickness. This was achieved by specifying high-strength concrete and casting each column from a single mix, thus avoiding settling of the aggregate. It is also worth noting that each column in the Great Workroom only supports relatively small loads, less than 40 m² of roof and snow. This is part of their elegance.

Lloyd's of London

Richard Rogers and Partners' design of the Lloyd's building in London is based around the idea that the building must be open to change and technological evolution. As such, the office floors have an overall thickness of 1,400 mm and contain two service voids for each floor of accommodation. Service elements that cannot be replaced easily, such as ductwork and lifts, are placed on the exterior of the building, away from the office environment. The internal spaces use a bespoke structural system based around an 1,800 mm concrete grid, supporting floors of highly serviced office spaces. As well as carrying the principle loads between columns, a grid work of 480 mm deep concrete beams contains extract vents and lunimaires, and provides the finished ceiling surface to office spaces. The metal panels of the luminaries can be removed easily to allow access to a 440 mm deep service void immediately above the principle structure. This void contains electrical wiring and the extract ducts, which carry stale air out of the building via the distinctive stainless steel ducts that line the façade. The void is continuous in all directions, allowing flexibility in future service routes. Concrete stubs sit on the nodes of the grid to support a 100 mm slab that carries the people and furniture of the floor above. This slab can afford to be so thin as it only ever spans the 1,800 mm between nodes. Above this slab lies another service void, which also runs unobstructed in all directions. This contains electrical, IT and communications equipment, as well as intake ducts supplying fresh air and an air-based space-heating system. The finished floor surface is provided by a raised floor made of 600 mm square panels. As with the ceiling panels, these can be temporarily removed to provide access to the service plenum. The structure is a mixture of in situ and precast concrete that has been carefully detailed to provide a uniform finish. The 1,100 mm diameter columns were cast in situ into steel moulds. Joints between casts are concealed by precast concrete 'yokes' that connect the columns to precast pre-stressed inverted U-shaped beams. The grid work spanning between the precast beams was cast in situ, but tight quality controls on site mean that the exposed soffits are visually indistinguishable between the two forms of construction. The thin slabs were cast into bespoke steel cassettes that act as permanent shuttering to the floors. The building bears a close resemblance to Rogers' earlier work, with Renzo Piano, in steel at the Pompidou Centre in Paris.

6.23 Lloyd's of London, completed in 1986
Designed by Richard Rogers and Partners

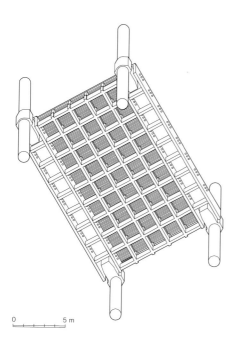

Column dimensions
1,100 mm diameter

Column type
In situ concrete with precast concrete nodes
connecting to the floor slabs

Grid
18,000 mm x 10,800 mm

Number of storeys
12

Floor loading
Light office use, 2.5 kN/m²

Resolution of wind loading
Bracing

6.24 Column and slab of
Lloyd's of London

0   5 m

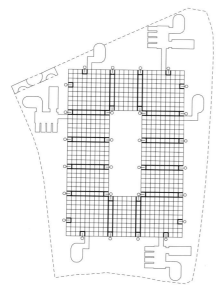

0   25 m

6.25 Typical floor plan of Lloyd's of London

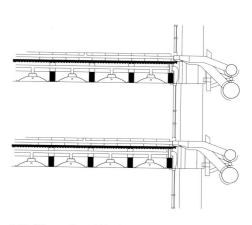

6.26 Edge section of Lloyd's of London – showing the
structure, air supply and return air

6.27 The curvilinear concrete slabs of Powergen Operational Headquarters
Architect: Bennetts Associates

Powergen Operational Headquarters

The Powergen Operational Headquarters building in Warwickshire, UK, by Bennetts Associates, was completed in 1995 and is one of the first office buildings in the country to make large-scale use of a concrete frame as part of an environmental strategy (FES). Arranged into two wings enclosing a central atrium space, the building exploits the thermal mass of concrete by exposing a concrete ceiling above open-plan office spaces. The structure is able to absorb heat from occupants and machinery during the day. At night, high-level windows allow in cool night air which purges the structure of the heat accumulated throughout the day. In order to maximise the surface area of the concrete soffit, the slabs were cast into coffers with an elliptical concave curve in section. Lighting rafts were then suspended beneath the coffers, in part to shine light upwards onto the concrete surface. The rafts also contained acoustically absorbent material, which helped control unwanted noise.

The open-plan wings of the building are supported by circular concrete columns with a diameter of 400 mm on a grid measuring 10,800 mm by 7,200 mm. Cross-bracing, located in separate service areas, helped to reduce the thickness of the columns. Edge beams span the shorter distances between the columns, with three coffers spanning the 10,800 mm length in each structural bay. The coffers were cast into GRP, with extruded rubber sections used to join the curved sections of mould, and aluminium strips used to join the flat edges. Along the length of the coffers, the aluminium joints can accommodate glass partitions should the occupants choose to change the interior in the future. The apparent thinness of the slab was achieved by post-tensioning the slab on site and increasing its depth towards the centre of its span. The angled profile is also thought to improve the refection of daylight into the centre of the plan. Post-tensioning also improved the appearance of the soffit by preventing any visible cracks. The slab is painted white, with two coats of standard emulsion, in order to improve the reflectance of the surface while exposing the concrete surface to the office environment.

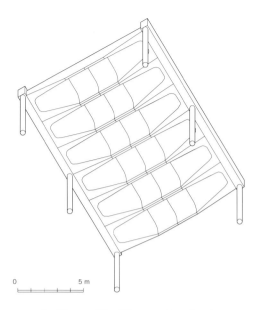

Column dimensions
400 mm diameter

Column type
In situ concrete

Grid
10,800 mm x 7,200 mm

Number of storeys
4

Floor loading
Light office use, 2.5 kN/m²

Resolution of wind loading
Cross-bracing

0   5 m

6.28 Curvilinear soffits of Powergen Operational
Headquarters' concrete floor slabs

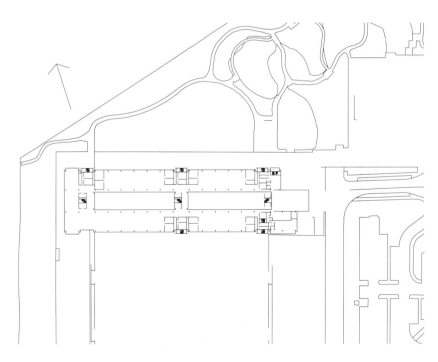

6.29 Typical floor plan of Powergen Operational Headquarters

7.1 The monolithic concrete wall of the core extension of the BBC's Broadcasting House on Portland Place, London – note the plywood inserts for future doors and services voids
Designed by MJP Architects

SEVEN **walls + blockwork**

'We would take that despised outcast of the building industry – the concrete block – out from underfoot or from the gutter – find a hitherto unsuspected soul in it – make it live as a thing of beauty – textured like trees. All we would have to do would be to educate the concrete block, refine it and knit it together.'
Frank Lloyd Wright[1]

Walls define space and provide performative qualities that range from basic shelter to sophisticated layered assemblies. Walls are generally vertical, except in the hands of specific contemporary architects. They have the potential to perform many tasks, from the prosaic, for example the core of the BBC's Broadcasting House extension (shown in Figure 7.1) which will become an almost unseen internal element, to the culturally significant, for example the precast concrete cladding of Nottingham Contemporary (see Figure 4.63, with its embedded memory of the lace industry). Walls can be divided by the structural role into:

- load-bearing; and
- non-load-bearing.

A specific structural role is for a wall to act as a retaining element or retaining wall, say retaining earth on a sloping site, as discussed in Chapter 5. In structural terms, a wall may be used in isolation, or in a monolithic construction in combination with the slabs, or as an infill to a framed structure. Internal walls can either be load-bearing or non-load-bearing, depending on the overall structural system of the building. Non-load-bearing walls are often described as partitions and are self-supporting, although they may have number of other performative requirements, for example providing acoustic and fire separation.

7.2 Frank Lloyd Wright's drawing of the 'First Block House', his title of a project for Harry Brown, Genesco, Illinois, 1906

The functional or performative potential of a wall includes:

- structural stability;
- enclosure;
- fire resistance;
- climatic modification;
- thermal insulation;
- acoustic isolation; and
- weather resistance.

The priorities of a wall's functions will vary according to its specific requirements. A wall may be constructed from a single multifunctional element, or as a composite of multiple monofunctional elements. In some situations, a monolithic concrete wall may be able to serve structural, thermal, acoustic, weather and fire requirements. Alternatively, functions may be broken down into various levels of complexity: the cavity wall, the insulated cavity wall, the non-load-bearing insulated cavity wall with an applied rainscreen, and so on.

Construction methods

A wall can be made from one of four primary construction methods: monolithic, masonry, framed, and membrane or stressed skin. Concrete wall construction is primarily either monolithic or masonry, although membrane and frame construction are also possible.

Masonry

A composite construction formed from blocks of various sizes and densities, masonry is usually laid in horizontal courses and bound by mortar. Concrete masonry units comprise concrete, light-weight concrete or aerated concrete, and can be manufactured with specific aggregates, providing a wide range of colours and finishes.

Monolithic construction

This consists of continuous castings, broken only by movement joints where necessary. With the correct mix, monolithic concrete has the potential to resist water penetration. As water will travel downwards on the surface of the wall, waterproofing is required at the head of any apertures to carry water away from this potential weak point. The expansion and contraction of monolithic elements requires an understanding of the causes and magnitude of movement, and joints need to be detailed accordingly. Considerations may include whether the element is in a stable thermal environment, or the scale of the concrete element and how it has been detailed structurally. Careful consideration is required as to whether the issue should be either detailed in or detailed out – a well-conceived detail will circumvent a problem rather than build it in.

Framed

Concrete can be used to form framed structures using in situ or precast sections. The frame is stabilised with cross-bracing or sheer walls, see Chapter 6 for a detailed description of concrete framed structures.

Stressed skin

The plasticity of concrete makes it eminently suitable for the fabrication of a shell structure, which gains its stiffness from the curvilinear form of the stressed skin (for further information see Chapter 8 on thinness and form).

Tilt-up construction

A specific means of constructing monolithic concrete walls is to cast them on the ground and tilt them up into position. Hence the term 'tilt-up construction'. Figures 7.3–7.5 show the construction of a house using the tilt-up method. The tilt-up slab house, in Venice, California, was designed by David Hertz of Syndesis as his family home. It has an exposed internal steel portal frame that is clad in white concrete panels, fair-faced on both sides and 150 mm thick. The key components of this cladding were cast on site and tilted up into position. Tilt-up construction was selected due to the tight site constraints. The units were cast horizontally with a perimeter shutter like a floor slab, and were then raised to the vertical. Units range in size from 3.5 m to 4.5 m wide.

Tilt-up construction may prove a successful route for the casing of monolithic concrete walls which have a variable mix through the cross-section, with dense, more waterproof, concrete to the outside and an insulative aggregate to the other side, which becomes the inner face.

7.3 Tilt-up slab house under construction
Designed by David Hertz of Syndesis

7.4 Tilt-up slab house

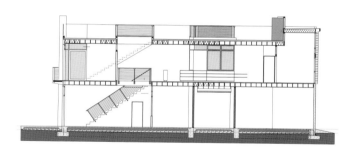

7.5 Tilt-up slab house:
long section and
first-floor plan

7.6 Peter Zumthor designed out the need for movement joints in the expansive terrazzo floor of Kolumba Art Museum by the use of underfloor heating powered by a geothermal source that keeps the slab and the conditioned spaces of the museum at a constant temperature

Movement joints

In situ concrete typically has a coefficient of thermal expansion in the range of 8–12 x 10^{-6}/°C. When designing monolithic reinforced concrete structures, structural continuity will be produced by the use of starter bars linking daywork or cold joints. Concrete shrinks as it cures and is subject to creep when loaded, so large in situ concrete structures may need movement joints to be provided to reduce the effects of temperature variations, shrinkage, settlement or creep. For reinforced concrete framed structures, movement joints of at least 25 mm should normally be provided at 50 m centres. These joints should be incorporated in the finishes and in the cladding at the movement joint locations. Aerated concrete blockwork has a coefficient of thermal expansion 8 x 10^{-6}/°C, and has a drying shrinkage of 0.09% when measured in accordance with BS 6073-1: 1981 *Precast Concrete Masonry Units*. As a guide it is not normally necessary to introduce movement joints in internal walls of blockwork unless the wall is about three times longer than its height. The specification of external cladding and internal linings, such as tilling, may influence the need for movement joins. The design of the complete wall should be considered holistically, taking into consideration all of the perfomative qualities that the wall needs to deliver.

Structural stability

In all structures it is essential to consider the effects of wind loading on the structural stability of the construction. In large-framed structures this can be achieved in two primary ways: by cross-bracing the end bays of each planar elevation, and by the introduction of stiff cores and shear walls. Lloyd's of London, by Richard Rogers, is an expressive example of a concrete structure stabilised by cross-bracing, whereas Silodam housing, by MVRDV, uses a concrete truss as a transfer structure above its integrated marina in Amsterdam harbour. Many office buildings are stabilised by a stiff in situ concrete core, which houses the lifts

7.7 Braga stadium, completed 2003
Architect: Souta de Moura Arquitectos

and provides fire compartmentation for the fire-escape stairs. It may be appropriate to stabilise a structure using sheer walls, and this strategy has been employed on a number of stadia, including Braga (see Figure 7.7; architects Souta de Moura Arquitectos with engineers AF Associados) and the new north stand of Ipswich Town's ground Portman Road (architects HOK Sport with engineers Jan Bobrowski and Partners). The shear walls of the new north stand were precast due to site constraints and the demands of a tight programme. The 14 shear walls are set at approximately 7.6 m centres and are over 11 m high and 3 m wide. Each wall supports the lower-racked tier and has steel I-beams cantilevered from the top of the structure of the upper tie and roof. For more information on this project, see *Concrete Quarterly*, Winter 2003.[2]

Blockwork

A block, unlike a brick, needs to be lifted with two hands. Typically, a concrete block is 215 mm high by 440 mm or 620 mm long, with an available range in thicknesses from 60 mm to 335 mm. For structural stability, concrete blocks are laid in a bonded pattern. Stack-bonded blockwork is possible if the mortar courses are reinforced with stainless steel mesh. Concrete blocks are a well-developed set of building components and the sizes are coordinated with other related materials, for example concrete blocks are manufactured to dimensions that match brickwork courses with face dimensions of 65 mm by 215 mm, the size of a typical cavity wall construction. Precast concrete lintels are also manufactured to coordinating dimensions for use with blockwork to avoid waste and cutting on site.

The architectural practice Team 4 was founded in 1963. It comprised Richard Rogers and his first wife Su as well as Norman Foster and his first wife Wendy. The house at Creek Vean was

7.8 The steps leading up to the entrance
of Creek Vean
Designed by Team 4

built for Su Rogers' parents, Marcus and Rene Brumwell, as a home for their retirement and was completed in 1966. Its relatively low-tech approach is distinct from the later work of Team 4. The linear plan is based around two axes, staged around views of Pill Creek and the Fal estuary, while also accommodating their modern art collection. The use of planting on the roofs and stairs make the exposed concrete blockwork walls appear buried into the steep slope, but the walls are in fact freestanding, with access from the road via a small bridge. Despite demands by the local authority for the walls to be externally painted, they remain as exposed blocks, internally and externally, with exposed concrete soffits and slate floors. Items of furniture, such as the bed of the master bedroom, are framed in cast reinforced concrete volumes. The house is listed Grade II* by English Heritage.

Despite it simple form of construction, both Norman Foster and Richard Rogers expressed frustration at the prolonged three-year building time, citing the project as motivation for rethinking their approach to construction methods. It is notable that concrete and concrete blocks, however, remained key components in their projects.

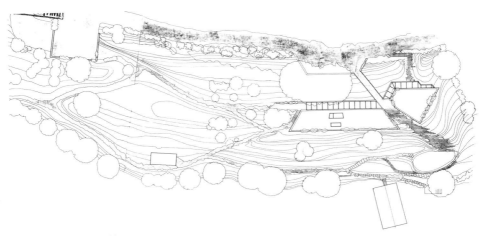

7.9 Site plan of Creek Vean

7.10 Creek Vean

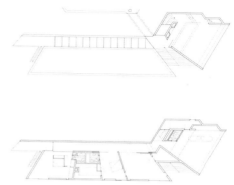

7.11 Floor plans of Creek Vean

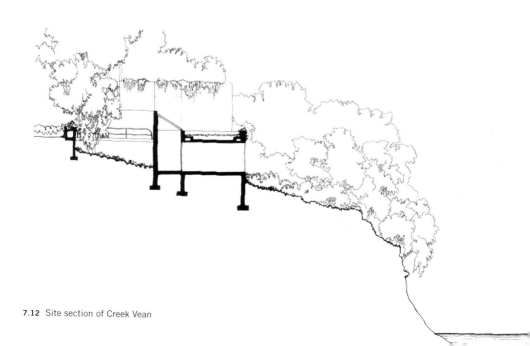

7.12 Site section of Creek Vean

7.13 Centraal Beheer Insurance Office
Architect: Herman Hertzberger

The Centraal Beheer Office building for an insurance company in Apeldoorn, designed by Herman Hertzberger and completed in 1972, is characterised by the use of fair-faced blockwork and exposed concrete. Hertzberger's aim was to use apparently humble and robust building materials to form a welcoming and open-ended architecture. Arnulf Lüchinger, in *Herman Hertzberger: Buildings and Projects*, examines the thinking behind this project:

'The idea ... is that of a building as a sort of settlement, consisting of a larger number of equal spatial units, like so many islands strung together. These spatial units constitute the basic building blocks; they are comparatively small and can accommodate the different programme components (or "functions"), because their dimensions as well as their form and spatial organization are geared to that purpose. They are therefore polyvalent ...

The basic requirements of an office building may well be simple enough in principle, but it was this need for adaptability that led to the complexity of the commission. Constant changes occur within the organization, thereby requiring frequent adjustments to the size of the different departments. The building must be capable of accommodating these internal forces, while the building as a whole must continue to function in every respect and at all times.'[3]

The modular fair-faced concrete blockwork is the physical embodiment of the architecture as well as the means of realising this architectural intent. During the 1970s and beyond, the use of fair-faced blockwork was often reproduced for its economy and robustness, unfortunately not always in the hands of skilful architects.

7.14 The atrium of Centraal Beheer

7.15 A meeting space off the atrium
of Centraal Beheer

The walls of the undercroft of Stansted Airport, designed by Foster Associates, comprise stack-bonded blockwork. The blocks were specially manufactured with frogs (an indentation on the top surface) to ensure that the blocks were always installed the same way up, thus creating an even and consistent texture to the walls, even though this is a non-public area within the airport.

7.16 Centraal Beheer, completed 1972

Acoustic isolation

Approved Document E of the Building Regulations (England and Wales) – *Resistance to the Passage of Sound* defines the performance requirements for elements of a building that should provide acoustic isolation, such as party walls and floors in houses and apartment buildings. To achieve acoustic isolation the main requirements are:

- mass within the construction which can absorb sound energy;
- continuity of construction – a tiny hole in a wall will result in a sound path that negates the performance of the construction; and
- separate layers that resonate at different frequencies and that are isolated by an air cavity.

Concrete can play a key part in providing acoustic isolation in an element such as a party wall in terrace housing. Approved Document E – known as Part E – defines the requirements for the resistance to the passage of sound of key constructional elements. This document sets out two methods for compliance with the Building Regulations on site sound testing after completion or by the use of robust details that are illustrated in the *Robust Details Handbook*.[4] These details have been tested and should achieve a level of sound insulation of at least 5 dB better than Part E requires.

For more information on detailing for acoustic insulation, see *How to Achieve Acoustic Performance in Masonry Homes*[5] and *The Robust Details Handbook*.[6]

Table 7.1: Minimum site test values for acoustic isolation to be achieved between purpose built dwelling houses and flats

	Airborne sound insulation[1] $D_{nT,w} + C_{tr}$	Impact sound insulation[2] $L'_{nT,W}$
Walls	45 dB	
Floors and stairs	45 dB	62 dB

Notes
1 For airborne performance, the higher the value the better the sound insulation
2 For impact performance, the lower the value the better the sound insulation

Table 7.2: Minimum site test values for acoustic isolation to be achieved between purpose built rooms for residential purposes

	Airborne sound insulation[1] $D_{nT,w} + C_{tr}$	Impact sound insulation[2] $L'_{nT,W}$
Walls	43 dB[3]	
Floors and stairs	45 dB	62 dB

Notes
1 For airborne performance, the higher the value the better the sound insulation
2 For impact performance, the lower the value the better the sound insulation
3 This value is slightly lower than the second insulation level allowed for dwelling houses and flats

Table 7.3: Fire resistance of walls built from concrete blocks manufactured using Class 1 Aggregates (courtesy of Cemex)

	Single leaf		Cavity wall	
	Load bearing	Non-load bearing	Load bearing	Non-load bearing
Solid dense				
90 mm	1 hr	2 hr (3 hr)	1 hr	6 hr
100 mm	2 hr	2 hr (3 hr)	6 hr	6 hr
140 mm	2 hr	4 hr (4 hr)	6 hr	6 hr
190 mm	2 hr	4 hr (6 hr)	6 hr	6 hr
215 mm	2 hr	6 hr (6 hr)	6 hr	6 hr
Cellular / hollow				
100 mm	2 hr	2 hr (2 hr)	4 hr	6 hr
140 mm	2 hr	3hr (4 hr)	4 hr	6 hr
190 mm	2 hr	4 hr (6 hr)	4 hr	6 hr
215 mm	2 hr	4 hr (6 hr)	4 hr	6 hr
Lightweight 1400				
100 mm	2 hr	2 hr (4 hr)	6 hr	6 hr
140 mm	3 hr	4 hr (4 hr)	6 hr	6 hr
Lightweight 1100				
100 mm	2 hr	2 hr (4 hr)	6 hr	6 hr
140 mm	3 hr	4 hr (4 hr)	6 hr	6 hr

Note: The minimum dimensions relate specifically to the cover dimensions stated in BS8110. The bracketed figures denote walls finished with not less than 13 mm of sand:cement or sand:gypsum (with or without lime) plaster or rendering on each face of a single leaf wall.

Fire resistance and compartmentation

Concrete is inherently non-combustible, with a surface spread of flame of Class O. Table 7.3 sets out the fire ratings for walls built of concrete blocks manufactured using class 1 aggregates. It indicates the thickness required for specific fire ratings that will be required to provide part of a fire safety strategy. Showing that a concrete construction can readily achieve a fire rating of four hours in accordance with BS EN 1992 (Part 1–2): *Structural Fire Design*. The minimum cover dimensions in in situ concrete construction for a given fire rating is stated in BS8110-1:1997 *Structural use of concrete*.

Lime hemp concrete

Lime hemp concrete has been developed to
meet a requirement for a form of construction
that has low embodied CO_2 and which traps
CO_2 in the fabric. In France it is typically
spray applied, whereas in Britain it has tended
to be used as infill in the form of blockwork.
Aukett Fitzroy Robinson Architects, with Lister
Beare Engineers, working with Limecrete
have developed lime hemp concrete blocks
for the walls of a Distribution Warehouse for
Adnams' Brewery in Southwold, Suffolk. The
external walls are 500 mm thick, with the lime
hemp concrete block exposed internally, with
brickwork or lime render as an external face.
Lime hemp concrete can provide a construction
method with excellent thermal performance
and low U-values, while also providing thermal
mass. More detail on concrete's excellent
thermal performance in this role is covered in
Chapter 10 on sustainability.

7.17 The Adnams' Brewery Distribution Warehouse
Designed by Aukett Fitzroy Robinson Architects with
Lister Beare Engineers

7.18 The lime hemp concrete block walls of the Adnams' Brewery Distribution Warehouse

8.1   Hagia Sophia, constructed in Constantinople as a church
between 532 and 537 AD

EIGHT **thinness + form**

'Solid bodies, stressed surfaces, and slender members form the three basic
elements of building available to nature and to man. A rock, and egg shell
or the trunk of a tree express these elements in the same way as do an
Egyptian pyramid, the dome of Hagia Sophia and the Eiffel Tower.'
Fred Angerer[1]

All building structures need to resist imposed
loads and resist the dead weight of the
structure itself. The form of the structure is one
of the primary decisions in the design process,
with the basis elements defined as:

* the solid body – as typified by masonry
  construction;
* stressed surfaces – such as shells and
  domes;
* skeletal with slender members – beams
  and columns that form the basis of framed
  construction.

A solid body element of construction will
have dimensions in all three axis of the
same magnitude, as characterised by a block
of stone or concrete. A surface structure
will have two dominant dimensions: length
and width, with the third much less which
is typically described as thickness of the
structure although it is normally the smallest
dimension. A flat concrete floor slab is a
good example. Slender members have a
dominant linear dimension, as characterised
by columns and beams. A building will rarely
adhere to a single principle of construction,
but rather will use a combination of these
forms.

Franz Hart, in *Hochbau konstrktion für
Architekten*, sets out this classification of
structure in the following statement:

'The differentiation between solid or
skeleton construction no longer applies
to two groups of building materials but
rather to two fundamentally different
methods of building construction.
Solid construction relies on a heavy
homogenous wall mass in which the
compression forces are uniformly
distributed. In the skeleton however
… the thin light framework of
bending-resistant members channels
the forces into single elements …
The development from solid body to
skeleton to panel can be followed not
only in methods of building but also
within individual building elements and
buildings: from the stone wall, through
the reinforced concrete skeleton to the
lightweight concrete slab; from the log
wall through the truss to the timber
framework; from solid vault through the
ribbed vault to the concrete shell; from
the one-way reinforced slab through
the T-beam and ribbed floor; from solid
plank door through the frame and infill
door to the flush plywood door. Building
aesthetic has created two polarities –
massive construction, be it member
construction or wall construction, and
frame construction – between which
all building methods find a place. If to
these two categories – solid mass and
soaring skeleton – is added a third, the

stressed surface, then many structures which cannot be included in either of the two earlier categories, and which therefore appear unusual, can be classified.'[2]

Having already examined frames (Chapter 6) and walls (Chapter 7), this chapter focuses on surface structures and the economy of means, combined with elegance, that architecture constructed from concrete can achieve.

Surface structures

Concrete is particularly suited for use in surface structures; its plasticity, when wet, will readily form complex curves and can respond directly to structural and spatial requirements. While, in this respect, there is a great deal of flexibility, the forms are still dependent on the constructional constraints of the formwork. Economy is dependent on the derivation of form and by methods of tessellation or panelisation of the formwork. The form of a concrete surface structure is a synthesis of spatial/structural factors and its means of construction. They can be considered both in terms of elements and as complete structures.

8.2   Primary structural typologies

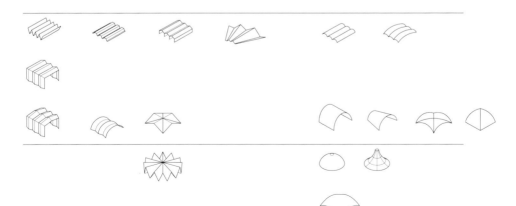

8.3   Basic typologies of surface structures, based on Angerer

A surface structure distributes either all or a large proportion of forces over its surface. Thin surfaces are capable of handling forces within their plane; bending forces, perpendicular to the plane, cannot be sustained. Surface structures, therefore, accommodate these forces by being shaped into a suitable form. One of the simplest forms for a surface structure is a folded plate structure. The potential stiffness created by folding a plane can be readily demonstrated by comparing the floppiness of a sheet of paper with the sheet after it has been folded into simple peaks and troughs. Stressed skin structures can be classified by either their geometric form – primary types are the developable surface, shell-folded or plate (Figure 8.2) – or by their load-bearing behaviour – beam, portal frame or arch.

Domes

The dome is the earliest form of a long-span structure. The Pantheon was built in 126 AD for Emperor Hadrian and this temple was covered by a dome with a span of 43 m, which was constructed in lightweight concrete. It was consecrated as a church five centuries later. The church of Hagia Sophia in Constantinople, constructed between 532 and 537 AD, is focused on a dome with a span of 30.5 m. Following the rediscovery of concrete in the nineteen century, it was possible, by 1913, for Max Berg to design the Jahrhunderthalle (Centennial Hall) for the Breslau Exhibition with a 65 m diameter dome. This ribbed dome springs from massive arches. For some historians of the Modern Movement, the clarity of Berg's dome is clouded by neoclassical elements.

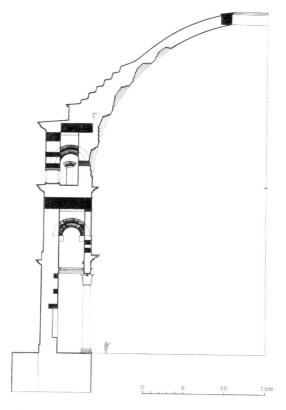

8.5 The coffered concrete dome of the Pantheon in Rome, completed 126 AD

8.4 Cross-section of the Pantheon in Rome

8.6 Sunshine reveals the 'earthy' concrete of the coffered dome of the Pantheon

8.7 Jahrhunderthalle (Centennial Hall) in Breslau, now Wroclaw, Poland, photographed in 2008
Architect: Max Berg

8.8 The ribbed reinforced concrete structure of the dome of the Jahrhunderthalle

8.9 The boardmarked concrete of the Jahrhunderthalle

Folded-plate

Folded-plate structures allow loads to be transferred inline with the plane, unlike slabs where the loading is perpendicular. The span, therefore, corresponds to the depth of the fold, allowing the plate thickness to be minimised. Owing to their flat surfaces, the formwork for fold-plate structures is generally simpler to construct than doubly curved shells. The geometric complexity of a doubly curved surface can be minimised by constructing it from a straight line or a rule surface, as demonstrated by the Chapel of Nôtre Dame du Haut in Ronchamp, architect Le Corbusier (see Figure 1.16). Potentially, the simplest curved surfaces are developable surfaces that can be formed from a flat sheet without cutting or folding.

Thin shells

A shell that gains all of its stiffness from a surface alone can be described as a 'monocoque structure'. Monocoque is the French for 'single shell'. If a shell structure is stiffened with ribs, it becomes a semi-monocoque structure.

8.11 An egg is a monocoque shell

Constructing thin shell domes

Potentially the most basic means of constructing a small concrete dome is to create the form of the dome in earth and cast the concrete directly onto this surface, which would typically be applied manually and smoothed using hand tools. Once the concrete is set, the earth is dug out leaving a concrete enclosure. A better method of dome building is to construct timber falsework or centring. It is thought that the Pantheon was built using concentric rings of masonry and wood toped by timber centring on which the concrete was cast.

8.10 Club Náutico (Maritime Club), Cuba (1953)
– photographed in 2006
Architect: Max Borges-Recio

A simple and cost-effective way of constructing a concrete shell structure is with a pneumatic formwork made up of triangular or trapezoidal pieces of fabric, which are welded or sewn together. In 1941, Wallace Neff was one of the first architects to design and construct a concrete shell using this method. The concrete shell construction begins with the air-form being tied down to a concrete foundation ring. The air-form is then inflated. Entry into the air-form is enabled by a double door air-lock. The pneumatic formwork can then be either removed and reconditioned for reuse or left in place depending on whether the concrete is sprayed onto both sides of the formwork.

In 1967, Dante Bini used pneumatic formwork to create concrete shells using a slightly different erection technique. He produced a 15 m high concrete shell at Colombia University in less than two hours by tying the pneumatic form onto a concrete base, laying a web of steel springs upon it and then pouring the concrete on top of the assemblage. The pneumatic form is then inflated and any irregularities in the concrete are smoothed out. To achieve a structurally sound form using this method, fibre reinforced concrete would have to be used and insulation applied after the concrete has set. Using fibre reinforced concrete is advantageous as the laying out of the reinforcing bars is the most time-consuming part of the construction process.

The design of shell structures and other structures with complex geometrical forms is facilitated by finite element analysis to establish the stresses within a structure and its potential stiffness. Finite element analysis, although now widely used in other fields, was developed to solve the complex problems of stiffness and structural performance in civil and aeronautical engineering; in essence, a finite element analysis software package finds approximate solutions to partial differential equations as well as integral equations. The form of

the structure may well be explored using digital geometric modelling, including the parametric modelling of a range of geometric options within the selected constrains. Both these processes can be used to optimise the structure and to understand its structural behaviour – optimum structural forms are not necessarily pure or Euclidian, nor are they formed from wilful geometry.

Jørn Utzon

Sydney Opera House
Jørn Utzon's inventive and sensitively crafted contribution to twentieth-century architecture is seminal in a discussion of thinness and form. As Kenneth Frampton observes in *Studies in Tectonic Culture*:

> 'Like Wright, Utzon has engaged structural form in ways that few architects have had the will or capacity for; for while architects invariably employ engineers to help them achieve large spans, few have elected to ground their primary expression in the spanning capacity of folded-slab construction. I refer here not only to Utzon's involvement with reinforced concrete shell construction, as is evidenced by the Sydney Opera House, but also his folded-slab roofs projected as post-tensioned long-span structures in reinforced concrete.'[3]

8.12 Sydney Opera House
Architect: Jørn Utzon; Structural engineer: Ove Arup

8.13 The precast concrete shells of the Sydney Opera House being erected on the in situ concrete podium

8.14 The precast concrete shells of the Sydney Opera House under construction

Frampton, in *Studies in Tectonic Culture*, gives an eloquent account of the geometrical development of the shell structures of the Sydney Opera House and how they progressed from gestural to the generational:

> 'Utzon would be occupied with their unresolved geometrical structure for almost four years before he finally happened on a solution that allowed him to produce arched segments of varying curvature from a range of precast modular units.'[4]

The generative geometry of the shells was found 'by cutting three sided segments from a sphere thus deriving regularly modulated curved surfaces from this solid', like segments cut from a round orange.[5]

Ove Arup described the structure of the Sydney Opera House to be a rare example of a structure 'where the best architectural form and the best structural form are not the same'.[6] Utzon rejected Arup's suggestions of forming the shells as a hybrid structure with steel ribs

8.15 The precast concrete ribs of the Sydney Opera House being clad with a tile faced precast concrete outer shell

with precast skins. Nor was the form of the shells readily analysed, as Arup observed: 'To replace the sails with rabbit-ears would be disastrous'.[7] It is Utzon's geometry, derived from a single sphere 75 m in diameter, that defines the tectonic of this opera house.

The Sydney Opera House is clad in off-white Swedish Höganäs ceramic tiles. Utzon insisted that these tiles were placed in the face of the moulds for the precast. He believed that only through prefabrication was it possible to achieve the level of accuracy necessary. He noted how the acuity of the human eye could detect imperfection on the surface of roofs designed on a civic scale. It is the selection of these tiles that imbues the Sydney Opera House with the quality to reflect the light and changing weather patterns of Sydney harbour.

The podium acts as grounding for the sail-like shells of the roof, and it also forms a vast column-free entrance space. This is achieved by an in situ concrete folded plate structure that clear spans 50 m. Frampton notes that 'with the bulk of the structural concrete section shifting from the bottom to the top as the effective bending moment shifted from positive to negative. Serving as a cranked profile for the concourse steps, this slab also acted partially as an arch.'[8]

The story of the Sydney Opera House is a sad tale of an architect who was badly treated by his client. Having deservedly won the international competition in 1957, Utzon never saw the completed project before he died in 2009. Yet his project has come to define the visual signature of Sydney and Australia. The link to Eero Saarinen, who died in 1961 aged only 51, is also important. Saarinen's completed projects have a strong correspondence with Utzon's architecture. Saarinen played a pivotal role in the jury of the Sydney Opera House, although some of this has past into architectural folk law – Saarinen drew

8.16 The structure of the podium of the Sydney Opera House

two perspectives of Utzon's entry, which are thought to be critical in explaining the scheme that became the winning entry. As Antonio Román suggests: 'Nevertheless, the affinity between the work of the two architects further underscores the likelihood of Saarinen's pivotal role in Utzon's selection.'[9]

Bagsvaerd Church – delight in the detail
Although it was completed in 1977, Bagsvaerd Church speaks poetically to the condition of architecture today. It combines simple industrial components with a parametrically

8.17 Bagsvaerd Church, photographed in 2009 – note the mature Silver Birch trees, planted shortly after completion in 1977
Architect: Jørn Utzon

8.18 Points of human contact are recorded and honoured by Utzon, as in this half-round ceramic tile toping an in situ concrete wall in the gallery of Bagsvaerd Church

8.19 The circulation of the church is organised by a 'thick-wall' plan, which are naturally lit by Velux industrial glazing

8.20 Blowholes in the self-finished in situ concrete of the frame of Bagsvaerd Church

generated geometry. It is only the glazed tiles on the external precast concrete panels that suggest the billowing cloud-like roof of the interior. Utzon conceived of the shells as clouds in a troubled celestial sky, as Frampton notes: 'the vaults at Bagsvaerd have a Baroque aura about them, particularly the way they modulate light'.[10] The forms of the vaults are generated by a series of internal and external circles extruded across the depth of the nave in a courtyard-based plan. The vaults are constructed from board-marked concrete shells spanning 18 m, which were sprayed from above. An independent waterproof roof of corrugated sheathing and industrial glazing complete the construction.

Circulation is organised in a thick-walled plan topped with simple industrial glazing, and here the in situ concrete frame of 300 mm square columns is expressed. This is the only concrete element to remain unpainted – it has an 'as-struck' quality, as typically the blowholes in the concrete are left untouched. Utzon, however, celebrates moments of human contact with the concrete, for example capping internal concrete walls in blue ceramic – 'this is were the hand passes'.[11]

Where the exterior of the church can be read as a simple industrial or agrarian building, the interior is a celebration in modulated light that adsorbs all of the variations in the passage of the sun and the weather conditions in this suburb of Copenhagen. Utzon exploits the form of the vaults exclusively for performative reasons; this is not an example of self-referential form making, which is commonplace in contemporary architecture. At Bagsvaerd Church, Utzon delights in the detail and demonstrates the depth of his tectonic understanding of space in light. Frampton honours Utzon's 'mastery over prefabrication in which he is able to exploit a modular productive system as a source of inspiration not limitation'.[12]

8.21 The board-marked sprayed concrete vaults form 'clouds' above the nave of Bagsvaerd Church

Jørn Utzon, in conversation, observed that 'this is an architecture that is enormously simple and straightforward and gives the building a feeling of totality'.[13] He continued to describe the vaults: 'They are injection moulded – the concrete is so fine that it is like the finest natural stone. And that technique then means you can achieve what is a beautiful thing in a church – the greatest simplicity and economy – economical in the use of materials because these cylindrical shapes are so rigid in themselves even though they are only 12–13 centimetres thick.'[14] The vaults span over 17 m across the courtyards of the thick-walled plan.

Thinness

Ove Arup, in his engineering of the spiral ramps of the penguin pool in Regent's Park Zoo, London (1934), demonstrated the potential for reinforced concrete to achieve slender and elegant structural forms. However, the limiting factors are the potential strength of the concrete mix and the need to provide adequate cover to the reinforcing bars, and so the desire to form structures that span further, using minimal material with an economy of means and potentially even greater elegance, has led to the development of fibre reinforced concrete. The fibres range from alkaline-resistant glass to polymers and steel. Ultra high-strength concrete and the use of steel fibres to achieve robust thin sections, including CRC and Ductal, are discussed in Chapter 2.

Glass-fibre reinforced cement

Developed in the 1960s, glass-fibre reinforced cement (GRC) is a composite material that combines alkaline-resistant glass fibres with sand and cement. The glass fibres provide the tensile strength to the composite and, unlike reinforced concrete, there is no need to add steel reinforcement, enabling components to be produced which are thinner and lighter. The skin of a GRC cladding panel will typically be between 6 mm and 18 mm. GRC is manufactured by one of two processes: spraying or premixing. Sprayed GRC is frequently used in the production of larger items, such as cladding panels, because it allows a fibre content of 5–6%, so it is stronger than premix (which is limited to 3–3.5%) and has a lower water content than premixed. The glass fibres must be alkaline resistant, otherwise the cement will erode the fibres and the structural integrity of the component will be lost.

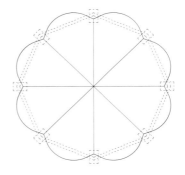

8.22 The GRC shell of Stuttgart Flower Hall
Designed by Hans Luz and Partners with
engineer Jörg Schlaich

8.23 Plan of Stuttgart Flower Hall

8.24 The GRC shells of Stuttgart Flower Hall on the
formwork prior to lifting

8.25 Valley detail showing the joining of two modules
with in situ GRC

8.26 A module being lifted into position

8.27 The completed Stuttgart Flower Hall

The shell structures of Stuttgart Flower Hall for the Garden Festival of 1977 were designed by engineer Jörg Schlaich with architects Hans Luz and Partners. This GRC shell structure has an average thickness of 15 mm and, as each segment weighs only 2,500 kg, each one could be craned into location. The shell was completed with in situ zones of GRC.

Raoul Bunschoten of Chora, with students at the London Metropolitan University, designed a GRC canopy for a pavilion for Homerton in east London. The design is based on a stiff freeform structure that would provide shelter. The voids in the semi-monocoque structure are an intrinsic part of the environmental performance of the pavilion. In order to test these ideas, a quarter-sized GRC prototype of the canopy was fabricated by second-year students at the London Metropolitan University under the guidance of the author. Extensive tests on the mix of GRC were undertaken by the students before the canopy prototype was fabricated.

8.28 A quarter-sized GRC prototype of semi-monocoque canopy fabricated by second-year students at the London Metropolitan University

8.29 Factory for Universal Oil Products
Designed by Piano and Rogers

8.30 Factory for Universal Oil Products
– under construction

The factory for Universal Oil Products in Tadworth, Surrey, was designed by Piano and Rogers and was built in 1973. It is clad in a GRC cladding system finished with a lime green paint. Richard Rogers noted that: 'The prefabricated structure, decking and large cladding panel system enabled the basic envelope to be completely watertight in a short time, allowing finishing and services trades to work under cover. .... Running costs are reduced by substantially increasing the thermal insulation value of the glass reinforced cement cladding-system.'[15] The doors within the GRC cladding system were designed by Chris Wilkinson and fold upwards to minimise their visual impact on the façades.

EMV Housing at Villaverde in Madrid, designed by David Chipperfield Architects, is clad with pinkish-brown GRC units, which are only 20–25 mm thick, yet span floor to floor. This pigmented GRC demonstrates the tonal range within a single mix, resulting from variations during manufacturing. This patination was actively sought by the architect.

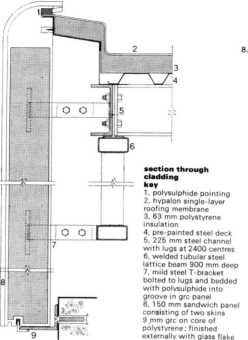

8.31 Factory for Universal Oil Products – working detail section and plan through the GRC cladding (original Piano and Rogers' working drawings)

section through cladding key
1. polysulphide pointing
2. hypalon single-layer roofing membrane
3. 63 mm polystyrene insulation
4. pre-painted steel deck
5. 225 mm steel channel with lugs at 2400 centres
6. welded tubular steel lattice beam 900 mm deep
7. mild steel T-bracket bolted to lugs and bedded with polysulphide into groove in grc panel
8. 150 mm sandwich panel consisting of two skins 9 mm grc on core of polystyrene ; finished externally with glass flake

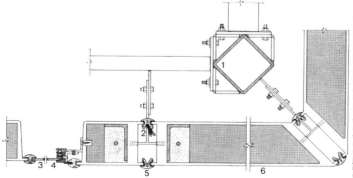

plan of cladding key
1. 152 mm square section tubular steel column turned on the diagonal to accommodate fixing of 175 mm beam end plates to collar
2. electrical wiring freeway
3. 6 mm float glass zipped into moulded nib of grc panel
4. anodised aluminium horizontal pivoting window bracketed to opening and sealed with neoprene compression gasket
5. neoprene friction-fit joint sealing profile inside and out
6. grc sandwich panel

8.32 EMV Housing at Villaverde, Madrid,
completed in 2005
Designed by David Chipperfield Architects

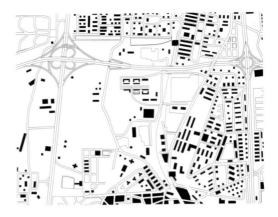

8.34 Figure Ground Plan of EMV Housing at Villaverde

8.33 GRC cladding of EMV Housing

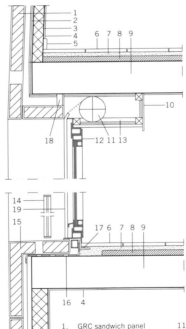

8.35 Sectional working drawing of the
GRC cladding of EMV Housing

1.	GRC sandwich panel	11.	Blind box
2.	30 mm polyurethane foam	12.	Aluminium double glazed
3.	Blockwork		windows
4.	Plaster	13.	Insulation
5.	Skirting board	14.	Balustrade
6.	Floor tiles	15.	GRC cill/GRC window cill
7.	30 mm mortar	16.	PVC waterproof membrane
8.	40 mm sand	17.	Mild steel angle
9.	Reinforced concrete slab	18.	Insulated plasterboard
10.	Architrave	19.	Blinds guides

Textile reinforced concrete

This is a development of fibre-reinforced cement using woven textile meshes, rather than chop strands. Textile reinforced concrete is more cementitious, as the maximum particle size is 1 mm, and a self-compacting additive is also used to ensure consolidation of the mortar around the fibre reinforcement. The fibres include:

- alkaline resistant glass;
- carbon fibre;
- aramide; and
- polypropylene.

Hartwig Schneider, Chair of Construction and Design at RTWH Aachen, designed and built the lamella arch (Figures 8.36–8.37) as a demonstration of the potential of textile concrete. The arch is formed by bolting together repeated diamond-shaped units.

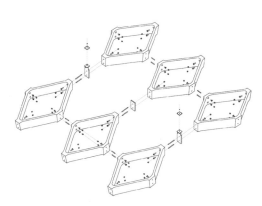

8.36 The precast textile component of the lamella arch

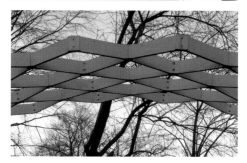

8.37 Lamella arch built from precast textile concrete components; the central image shows the textile reinforcement in the closed mould

9.1 Fukubu Hall
Architect: Tadao Ando

NINE **detail**

'I try to consider the intimate relations between material and form and between volume and human life.'
Tadao Ando[1]

The details of exposed concrete and the overall expression of the architecture are very directly linked. This is not, however, a limitation. The projects in this book illustrate just some of the diversity of outcomes that are possible.

9.2   House in Chur
Architect: Patrick Gartmann

Edge details

A fundamental source of the beauty of concrete is its plasticity. Although the possibilities are almost limitless, like all technology the casting of concrete has limits and constraints. The shuttering must be strikeable or the precast unit must be able to be removed from the mould. Therefore, the details for in situ concrete need to reflect the disassembly of the formwork and in precast the direction of the removal of the component, which should incorporate a draft angle to aid release and, typically, undercuts are not possible. How fine an edge is it possible to form? The limiting factor is the size of the aggregate and whether the surface of the cast concrete is to be removed. Guidance in Eurocode 2: Design of Concrete Structures (BS EN 1992-1-1:2004) recommends the use of a standard 25 mm chamfered edge detail, as it is more tolerant of aggregate placement. If a 90 degree corner is formed there is a risk of exposed aggregate as the stones may bridge across the corner. Therefore, the smaller the aggregate size, potentially the crisper corners can be. However, there is a risk of such corners eroding, as can

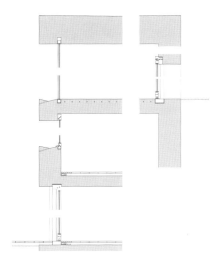

9.3   Section of House in Chur:
- roof – 600–660 mm insulating concrete to falls, sealed with two part fine stopper
- external walls – 450 mm insulating concrete
- windows and doors – double glazing in timber frames

be seen on some of the Sverre Fehn projects, especially where the comers are exposed to the extremes of Norwegian winters. The use of fibres will reinforce edges and allow thinner sections to be successfully cast, as discussed in Chapter 8. As a general rule, it is easier to create crisp corner details in precast rather than in in situ concrete. That said, it is possible, even when specifying in situ concrete, to produce almost rectilinear corner details, although there also is a risk that the leading edge will be lost when the formwork is struck. Patrick Gartmann's house in Chur demonstrates that, in the Swiss context, it is possible to form very crisply detailed concrete. Many of the details of this house have been developed to maintain the rectilinear expressiveness of the design – a good example of this is the falls of the window reveals, draining towards the window and away via weep holes.

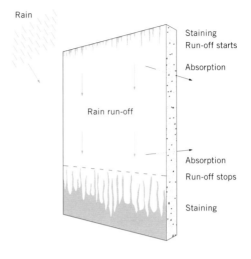

9.4   Diagram of weathering and staining

Weathering

The interaction of atmospheric and environmental conditions with the material characteristics, design and detailing of a building is known as weathering. It may be classified into two categories of action:

- physical – wind, rain, freeze thaw; and
- chemical – reactions between rainwater, atmospheric pollution and surface materials to produce oxidation and chemical deposition.

If a construction is continuously wet as a result of other details focusing rain onto it, the growth of *biological* organisms, such as moss and lichen, will occur.

Concrete responds directly to weathering, and its use in large uninterrupted surfaces makes these changes more apparent. Unless detailed carefully, undesirable results may appear within a short space of time. Rainwater is largely responsible for the uneven distribution of staining over a surface. Water removes and carries dirt, creating a cleaning action in some areas and a depositing action in others. In highly moulded concrete façades, careful consideration needs to be made of how the water will flow over that façade. The Ricola-Europe SA, Production and Storage Building at Mulhouse, designed by Herzog and de Meuron, uses the water staining of the concrete façade as the means of creating strong vertical patterning to the façade. Consideration also needs to made if a number of materials are used in conjunction with exposed concrete, for example the patination from copper cladding, as copper oxides, if they are allowed to flow over the concrete in rainwater, will stain the concrete green. Another example of the risk of staining concrete is oak cladding or decking above a concrete surface, as tannins are washed out of the oak by rainwater, staining the concrete dark brown to black.

9.5 Herzog and de Meuron took on the challenge of concrete responding to its environment – the water staining the concrete forms the patterns of the façades of Ricola-Europe SA, Production and Storage Building at Mulhouse

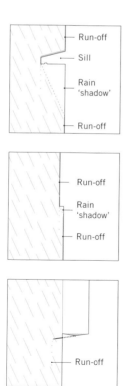

Run-off

Sill

Rain 'shadow'

Run-off

Run-off

Rain 'shadow'

Run-off

Run-off

9.6 Weathering details

9.7 Stone sill on the end of a terrace house in Bath showing staining from the water run-off and shelter from the sill

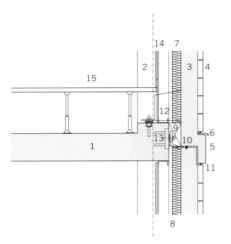

1 In situ concrete floor slab
2 Precast concrete column
3 Precast concrete cladding panel
4 50 mm sandstone
5 Polished pre cast concrete string course
6 Stainless steel drip profile
7 Insulation
8 Vapour barrier
9 Fire barrier
10 Inner compression seal
11 Outer wet seal with weepholes
12 Load bearing panel fixing
13 Head restraint panel fixing
14 Plasterboard lining
15 Raised access floor

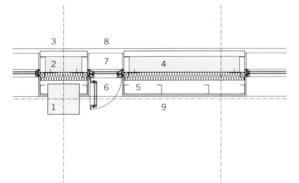

1 Precast concrete column
2 Precast concrete cladding panel
3 50 mm sandstone
4 Insulation
5 Vapour barrier
6 Aluminium window
7 Aluminium window cill
8 Stainless steel drip profile
9 plasterboard lining

9.8 Note the stainless steel drip section that prevents
the sandstone-faced precast concrete panels
of the Potterrow Development for the University of
Edinburgh staining and getting too wet
Architect: Bennetts Associates

9.9 Potterrow Development
viewed from George Square

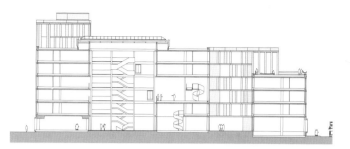

9.10 Potterrow Development – section through the Informatics Forum

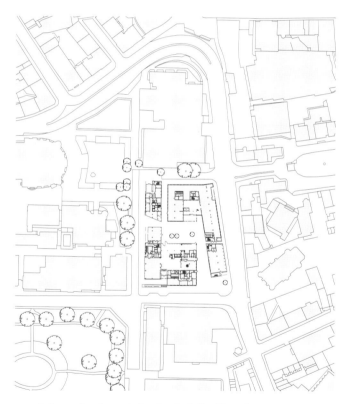

9.11 Potterrow Development site plan, including Phase 2

9.12 The casting of the stone-faced precast cladding of Potterrow Development

9.13 Weathered board marked concrete of Sverre Fehn's Norwegian Glacier Museum Fjærland, which was completed in 1991, photographed in 2010. Note the smooth shuttered concrete with an expressed protruding v-joint on the concrete walls of the south facade

External concrete surfaces that are horizontal or near the horizontal, such as roofs, wall tops and sills, need to be sealed to avoid the ingress of moisture. Separate components, such as membranes, copings and sill plates, can be used to prevent this. If an exposed surface is required, a sealant must be applied, such as an epoxy resin or a polymer modified cement slurry. Larger horizontal surfaces can also accumulate significant quantities of dirt from the atmosphere and the surrounding area, and this should be considered in the detailing, for example draining back towards the façade and out via concealed gutters.

Thermal insulation

Global warming threatens the well being of humankind and is a product of our own industry.[2] As discussed in Chapter 10 on sustainability, it is essential that the built environment is designed so that less CO_2 (one of the main greenhouse gasses) is produced. The Building Regulations have taken steps towards reducing the CO_2 emissions from construction with the aim of enabling Britain to achieve its Kyoto protocol targets and to meet the requirements of the European Union's Energy Performance of Buildings Directive (EPBD). The design of the environmental performance of buildings should be considered holistically and is not just a matter of achieving low U-values. The air-infiltration rate of the fabric needs to be considered in order to minimise unwanted air changes or drafts. In the PassivHaus standard, this rate is less than 1 $m^3/h/m^2$ tested at 50 Pascals; this is 10 times stricter than the standard in Approved Document L1A

9.14 Flower kiosk at Malmo Eastern Cemetery,
completed in 1969
Architect: Sigurd Lewerentz

of the Building Regulations for England and
Wales. A low air-infiltration rate is achieved by
specifying an appropriate breather membrane
and by carefully detailing all junctions,
so that good workmanship can be readily
accomplished. When combined with a well-
insulated construction, comfortable conditions
can be achieved readily. All elements need to
contribute to this air-infiltration rate, particularly
windows and doors. A key early design question
is orientation and the provision of good daylight;
getting the benefit of passive solar gain while
avoiding glare are key factors. The benefits of
thermal mass are set out in Chapter 10.

In the Building Regulations for England and
Wales, thermal performance for new dwellings
is set out in Approved Document L1A, 2010.
Table 9.1 contains outline guidance on
elemental U-values that comply with Part
L, which are described in the document as

9.15 Close up of the in situ concrete of Lewerentz's
flower kiosk, photograph taken in 2009

Table 9.1: Outline guidance limiting U-values for thermal insulation in dwellings, based on Part L1A, 2010

Limiting fabric parameters	
Roof	0.20 (W/m²K)
Wall	0.30 (W/m²K)
Floor	0.25 (W/m²K)
Party Wall	0.20 (W/m²K)
Windows, roof windows, glazed rooflights, curtain walling and pedestrian doors	2.0 (W/m²K)
Air permeability	10 m³/h/m² at 50 Pascals

'the worst acceptable standards for fabric properties'.[3] The 2010 version of 'Part L' encourages the specifying architect to achieve better lower U-values by using Target CO_2 Emission Rate (TER). However, why such a gap has been left between the Building Regulations and the voluntary Code for Sustainable Homes (CSH) is a mystery and a tragedy.

Thermal performance of concrete

Concrete that is made with a dense aggregate typically has a thermal conductivity of around 1.2 W/mK and a density of about 2,200 kg/m³, resulting in poor insulative performance with high thermal mass. Therefore, if insulation is used, its relationship to the concrete can be considered to minimise conductivity and utilise thermal mass.

As concrete is often suited to continuous construction and cantilevers, achieving a continuous layer of insulation requires careful detailing. Thermal bridging not only allows energy to be lost, but can also lead to the condensation, staining and mould growth, all of which can be avoided by careful detailing when placing the insulation and the use of thermal breaks.

Insulation placement strategies

Where should the insulation be placed? The options are shown in Figure 9.16:

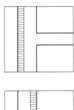

9.16 Insulation placement strategies

- external insulation;
- internal insulation;
- insulating cores can be used with both in situ and precast concrete; and
- insulating aggregates and or active insulation.

Each option is discussed in this chapter, with selected project examples.

Table 9.2: Concrete-based wall details with thermal performance criteria

Full fill cavity wall: 100 mm block and 100 mm block (aircrete) with render	Solid masonry wall: 215 mm block (aggregate) mineral fibre insulation and reinforced render	Solid masonry wall: 215 mm block (aircrete), extruded polystyrene and reinforced external render	Precast concrete sandwich panel (70 mm/125 mm concrete)
Aircrete block ($\lambda = 0.15$)	Aggregate block ($\lambda = 1.13$)	Aircrete block ($\lambda = 0.15$)	Dense concrete ($\lambda = 1.83$–2.0)
Mineral wool ($\lambda = 0.033$)	Mineral fibre ($\lambda = 0.04$)	Extruded polystyrene ($\lambda = 0.029$)	PIR insulation ($\lambda = 0.023$)
300 mm wall (75 mm insulation) $U = 0.28$ W/m²K	360 mm wall (120 mm insulation) $U = 0.28$ W/m²K	300 mm wall (60 mm insulation) $U = 0.28$ W/m²K	295 mm wall (75 mm insulation) $U = 0.28$ W/m²K
325 mm wall (100 mm insulation) $U = 0.22$ W/m²K	375 mm wall (135 mm insulation) $U = 0.25$ W/m²K	325 mm wall (85 mm insulation) $U = 0.22$ W/m²K	325 mm wall (105 mm insulation) $U = 0.21$ W/m²K
350 mm wall (125 mm insulation) $U = 0.20$ W/m²K	420 mm wall (180 mm insulation) $U = 0.20$ W/m²K	340 mm wall (100 mm insulation) $U = 0.20$ W/m²K	330 mm wall (110 mm insulation) $U = 0.20$ W/m2K
375 mm wall (150 mm insulation) $U = 0.18$ W/m²K	440 mm wall (200 mm insulation) with aircrete block $U = 0.20$ W/m²K	375 mm wall (135 mm insulation) $U = 0.16$ W/m²K	370 mm wall (150 mm insulation) $U = 0.15$ W/m²K
375 mm wall (150 mm insulation) with low conductivity wall ties $U = 0.17$ W/m²K	480 mm wall (240 mm insulation) $U = 0.15$ W/m²K	385 mm wall (145 mm insulation) $U = 0.15$ W/m²K	375 mm wall (155 mm insulation) $U = 0.14$ W/m²K
400 mm wall (175 mm insulation) with low conductivity wall ties $U = 0.15$ W/m²K	615 mm wall (215 mm insulation) $U = 0.1$ W/m²K	415 mm wall (175 mm insulation) with aggregate block $U = 0.15$ W/m²K	440 mm wall (220 mm insulation) $U = 0.1$ W/m²K
500 mm wall (275 mm insulation) with low conductivity wall ties $U = 0.1$ W/m²K		515 mm wall (215 mm insulation) with aggregate block $U = 0.1$ W/m²K	

Code for Sustainable Homes

When designing a low-energy home, the key starting point is to specify a very low U-value for the walls, roofs and floors. Specifying a low U-value or super-insulation of about 0.1 W/m²K adds only a modest cost to the construction of a new build project. This needs to be coupled with a low air-infiltration rate, which is a question of specifying a fully taped breather membrane and carefully detailing all junctions, so that good workmanship can be readily achieved. A carefully detailed internal monolithic concrete structure is an alternative means of achieving a very low air-infiltration rate – rigorous detailing of all junctions remains vital.

The next key decision is orientation, in order to maximise beneficial solar gains and visual amenity, this needs to be combined with high-performance glazing. There is now a body of research and practice on achieving carbon neutral homes, however, there are still too few good examples. The Code for Sustainable Homes, launched in December 2006, is the UK Government's standard for assessing the environmental impact of new homes against a range of one to six stars. Although the Code covers nine categories of environmental impact, it is the ambition that all new homes should be 'zero carbon' from 2016. Concretes can significantly contribute to achieving a Code Level 6 or 'zero carbon'. This is set out in *Energy and CO₂: Achieving Targets with Concrete and Masonry*,[4] however, Table 9.2 extends the range of options down to 0.1 W/m²K. Steady state calculations of thermal resistance or U-values can be simply undertaken using a spreadsheet for any appropriate combination of materials as long as the thermal resistance (K-values) and thickness are known.

External Insulation

The placement of insulation outside the structure simplifies structural connections, as the structure is entirely contained within the insulating envelope, while adding complexity to the external envelope. External insulation

9.17 Werner House
Architect: Berth and Deplazes

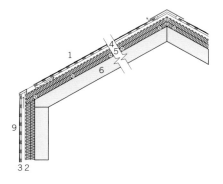

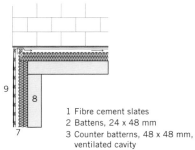

1 Fibre cement slates
2 Battens, 24 x 48 mm
3 Counter batterns, 48 x 48 mm, ventilated cavity
4 Secondary waterproofing (sarking)
5 120 mm thermal insulation and battens
6 Concrete roof
7 Airtight membrane
8 Concrete wall
9 Fibre cement board cladding

9.18 Details of Werner House showing the internally exposed concrete, insulation and fibre cement cladding

9.19 The Graduate Centre of London Metropolitan University
Architect: Studio Daniel Libeskind

9.20 The exposed internal in situ concrete walls of the Graduate Centre

the occupants. Externally, the insulation will need to be protected by a breather membrane and outer cladding.

Examples of externally insulated projects include the Graduate Centre of London Metropolitan University, designed by Daniel Libeskind and completed in December 2003, which is protected by stainless steel rain screen cladding, and the Centre for Sustainable Energy Technologies (CSET) building on the University of Nottingham's Ningbo campus in China, designed by Mario Cucinella with environmental design by Professor Brain Ford. CSET was completed in November 2008. The project uses internally exposed ggbs-based concrete for thermal mass, which is over clad with insulation that is protected from weathering by translucent glazing. The CSET building provides laboratory, office and seminar accommodation, and has been designed to serve as an exemplar building,

9.21 CSET building on the University of Nottingham's Ningbo campus in China
Designed by Mario Cucinella Architects

with an exposed concrete structure internally has the advantage that the thermal mass of the concrete can be used to store thermal energy. The thermal mass will respond to the interior climate, absorbing heating and cooling. In order to utilise this thermal mass, the surface of the concrete must remain exposed and visible to

demonstrating the state-of-the-art techniques for environmentally responsible, sustainable construction and energy efficient internal environmental control. It has been designed to minimise its environmental impact by promoting energy efficiency, generating its own energy from renewable sources, and using locally available materials with low-embodied energy wherever possible. It responds to diurnal and seasonal variations in ambient conditions by means of a five-point environmental design strategy:

- high performance envelope;
- exposed thermal mass;
- daylight and solar control;
- natural ventilation to tower; and
- ducted ventilation to laboratory and workshop.

Mario Cucinella designed the building 'to minimise the need for additional energy for heating, cooling and ventilation. In fact, the residual heating, cooling and ventilation load is estimated to be so low that this residual load, plus demand for electrical power for computing, lighting will be met from renewable energy sources.'[5]

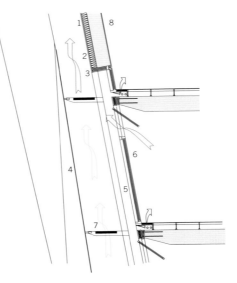

1 15 mm layer of plasterboard on adhesive
2 Mineral wool insulation
3 Vapour control layer
4 External fixed translucent glass facade
5 RHS steel column
6 Double-glazed unit with opening vent
7 Secondary steel structure to support maintenance walkway
8 ggbs based concrete

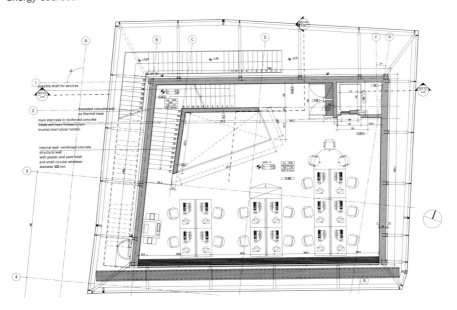

facing page

9.22 Façade detail of the CSET building on the University of Nottingham's Ningbo campus in China

9.23 Second-floor plan of the CSET building

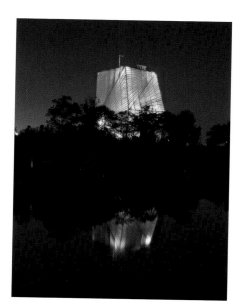

9.24 Night view of the CSET building, revealing its fidelity to the concept of a Chinese lantern

9.25 Inside the double façade

9.26 The Pod viewed from Bottle Lane, Nottingham
Designed by Benson and Forsyth Architects

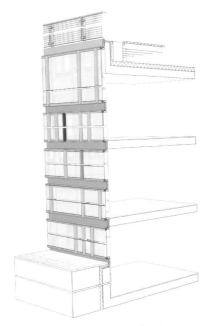

9.27 Benson and Forsyth Architects' design development drawing of the curtain walling of the Pod, which is specific to Bottle Lane

Concrete frames and curtain walling

The freedom offered by a frame structure led to the development of curtain walling, where the glazing and cladding only supports itself and typically spans from slab to slab. Since the 1950s curtain walling has become one of the most popular means of cladding, particularly for offices and mix-use projects. The Pod, a mixed-use scheme in Nottingham city centre, designed by Benson and Forsyth Architects, is an exemplar of how to design an aluminium and steel curtain walling that is fixed back to a concrete frame. When fixing curtain walling back to a concrete frame, it is essential to allow for the tolerance of the concrete, which is significantly greater than that of the curtain walling system. In the 1970s Schmidlin introduced cast steel components to accommodate these tolerances in three planes: vertically, horizontally and in plan. To aid this

9.28 The interior of the Pod, showing the relationship of the concrete frame and the curtain walling system

1. Galvanized mild steel parallel flange channel,
   30mm dense insulation,
   EPDM,
   Anodised aluminium flashing

2. Vertical Fin Anodised aluminium caps over steel pressure plates,
   Glazing Jansen 'Viss' System
   Steel curtain wall profiles, Galvanised & MIO painted

3. 152 x 152 mm I sections to span full height, fixed to structural
   frame via resin bolts.

4. Hydrotech roofing system,
   120 mm insulation,
   60 mm gravel
   Timber decking.

5. In-situ RC slab and up stand,
   Waterproofing system,
   200 x 200 steel base plate,
   'Tuning Fork' base connection,
   Orsogril balustrade panelling,
   Aluminium flashing.

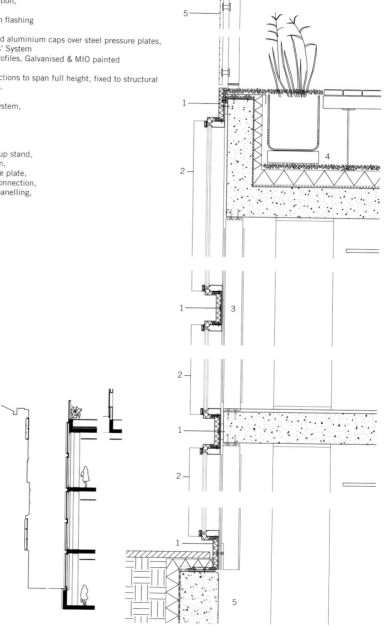

9.29 Section and working drawing of the curtain
walling of the Pod on Bottle Lane

9.30 The Royal Playhouse, Copenhagen – opened in 2008
Designed by Lundgaard & Tranberg Arkitekter

interface, Halfen or similar fixing channels should be cast into the concrete structure, onto which the cast or fabricated brackets of the curtain walling can then be fixed.

Internal insulation

Internal insulation allows for an exposed concrete exterior as the visible architecture, simplifying the external envelope. Structural connections, however, will need to be thermally broken. Internal insulation has the advantage that the lining system can take services and has strong architectural potential, however, this will effectively isolate the mass of the concrete and it cannot be used to store thermal energy.

Double skin core insulation

A number of projects incorporate insulation within a double concrete wall – this has the benefits of making the concrete available as thermal mass and the U-value can be taken to

9.31 The Royal Family of Denmark's entrance into the Playhouse

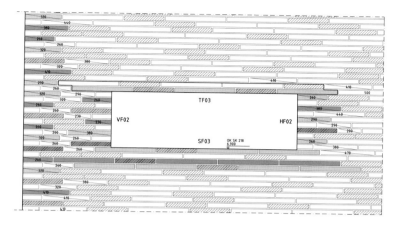

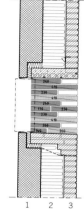

1   200 mm exposed
    reinforced concrete
    internal walls
2   200 mm insulation
3   150 mm deep
    handmade bricks

9.32 Detail of the window openings of the Royal Playhouse, Copenhagen

a very low value. When using in situ concrete this is a relatively expensive option, as the shuttering must accommodate and support the insulation or be cast in two stages. As both faces are non-combustible, the insulation can be a high performance foamed polymer. The width of construction will tend to increase due to the double skin. Sufficient width should be provided in each leaf between the rebar to allowing for the compacting tool or self-compaction concrete can be used. Owing to an increase in materials and complication in the process, double skins tend to be a more expensive option and may be most appropriate where a robust construction is required. To simplify the casting and formwork procedure, a precast concrete exterior can be hung from an in situ concrete structure, incorporating a layer of insulation or an insulated precast panel, such as Hardwall, could be specified, see Figure 9.38.

A three-storey concrete schoolhouse in Paspel was designed by Valerio Olgiati to appear as a whole, rather than an accumulation of forms. For this reason it conveys the appearance of a monolithic structure. The building essentially consists of two concrete parts, which form a double layer envelope. The concrete walls and floor slabs that form the internal layer create an independent load-bearing frame, which is then pinned back to the enclosing fare-faced concrete outer layer using individual shear pins. The two leafs support one another and only touch when they are joined by the shear connectors. All the joints between the walls and floor slabs are defined by shadow joints.

The external façade of the building conveys the treatment of the various working spaces and corridors within the building. The wood-lined internal classrooms have large windows with deep reveals which are flush with the inner

9.33 School in Paspels
Architect: Valerio Olgiati

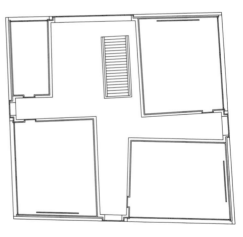

9.35 A second floor plan of the School in Paspels

9.34 Interior of the School

face and positioned to frame distinct views of the landscape. The location of the corridors and stairwells is conveyed by windows that are flush with the outer face to allow for optimum natural lighting. In addition, the cruciform layout of the plan enables the ingress of natural lighting from all directions, creating changing spatial effects throughout the day.[6]

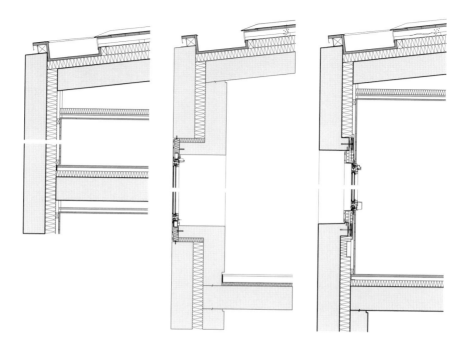

9.36 Sectional details of the School in Paspels showing: the timber lining; the double concrete wall at a window; and the timber lining at a window

Precast sandwich panels

Precast concrete sandwich panels comprise an outer layer of concrete, a layer of insulation and a backing leaf of concrete. They offer a reliable and cost-effective route to providing low U-values and thermal mass. Only the internal leaf is considered to act structurally. Sandwich panels combine structure fare-faced finishes and insulation in one component. These prefabricated products offer a significantly reduced site time as well as factory-based quality. The two concrete skins of the panels are tied together using preparatory ties with a very low coefficient of thermal conductivity, which are manufactured from a combination of fibre reinforced composites and polycarbonate (see Figure 9.38).

A number of manufacturers have introduced precast concrete sandwich panels, for example Trent Concrete's system is called Hardwall. The two skins of concrete are linked by carbon fibre pultruded composite connectors (the trade name is Thermomass), which minimise thermal transmission and were developed in the USA. The core comprises extruded polystyrene insulation. Panels are offered up to 4.1 m by 10 m. A 395 mm thick Hardwall panel includes 120 mm of extrude polystyrene insulation, providing a U-value of 0.28 w/m^{2}K. It is possible to specify U-values below 0.1 W/m^{2}K by using a thicker Hardwall panel. These panels offer a combination of excellent resistance to the passage of heat and accessible internal thermal mass.

9.37 J C Decaux's building was one of the first projects to use Hardwall in the United Kingdom
Architect: Foster and Partners

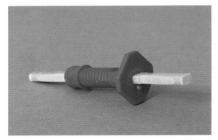

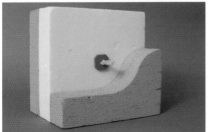

9.38 Hardwall connector and cut away
sample of a Hardwall panel

Insulating aggregates

Demands on insulative performance frequently prohibit the use of the truly monolithic concrete walls for use as the building envelope. However, as concrete is a composite itself, its own components have the potential to be tailored for more specific performance requirements, for example high-strength cements or insulating aggregates in design-specific matrixes. To achieve both an exterior and interior exposed surface, without the complications of a double skin, hollow-insulating aggregates can be used to improve the insulation value of a single continuous casting. The relatively poor insulation performance will result in large thicknesses, say over 400 mm. This massiveness of construction and the potential it provides at openings is clearly enjoyed by some architects. Materials such as foamed glass, perlite beads, exfoliated vermiculite or expanded clay aggregate may be used. The use of insulating aggregates is still in an experimental stage and should be carefully specified, and specific tests must be carried out to achieve the performance required, in terms of insulation, workability and structure. For example, certain mixes may allow hollow aggregates to float upwards to give an uneven insulation level and may compromise structural performance. Incorporating insulative materials in the concrete mix is an option demonstrated by Patrick Gartmann's house in Chur and the Double Church of Two Faiths by Kister Scheithauer Gross Architekten.

The house in Chur, Switzerland, is sited within a development plan prepared by Bearth and Deplazes (see Figures 9.2 and 9.3). It has a crisp rectilinear expression, however, the remarkable quality of this house is its use of monolithic concrete that achieves a reasonable U-value. The mix, developed by Gartmann, replaces sand with expanded glass and gravel with expanded clay. The 450 mm thick walls provide a U-value of approximately 0.58 w/m²K, and the roof slab, which is between 600 mm and 650mm thick, with a U-value of approximately 0.4 w/m²K. There is no internal insulation, nor internal plaster. Even the roof is waterproofed using a plastic modified cement slurry. This house appears to represent a potential starting point for the development of concrete mixes that provide structural and insulative properties.

St Maria Magdalena in Risefeld near Freiburg, Germany, which was built in 2002–04, is known as the Double Church of Two Faiths, as it contains a Catholic and a Protestant church. The competition to build the church was won by Kister Scheithauer Gross Architekten, who combined the two churches into a signal architectural entity, as, in the words of Professor Susanne Gross, 'the individual volumes of both churches seem too small to us compared to the size of the [public] square, we decided to consolidate

9.39 The Double Church of Two Faiths
Designed by Kister Scheithauer Gross Architekten

1 Entrance yard	5 Protestant church
2 Central hall	6 Catholic parish hall
3 Baptismal area	7 Kitchen
4 Catholic church	8 Small foyer

9 WC	13 Alcove for prayer
10 Northern chapel	14 Catholic church entrance
11 Catholic church sacristy	15 Southern chapel
12 Vestment area	16 Church shop

17 Protestant church sacristy	
18 Protestant church entrance	

9.40 Plans of the Double Church of Two Faiths

both churches into a homogenous form'.[7] The building has an irregular plan and can function either as two churches or one larger ecumenical congregation. The plan is divided by large moving concrete walls. Kristin Feireiss describes the interior of the

church as 'a sculpturally moulded room with the spaciousness of extended marquees, a structure made completely of concrete which radiates fragility, a spatial experience which has Louis Khan-like dimensions'.[8] The external envelope and structure of the

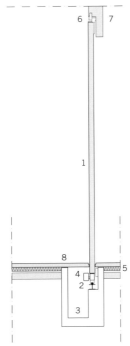

1 Moveable wall element, wall thickness
   180 mm, in situ concrete
2 Steel wheel on steel profile with guide
3 Service shaft
4 Electric drive
5 Sound absorption
6 Guide run of guide pulley
7 Wall-like support, in situ concrete
8 Smooth-finish concrete floor

9.41 Door detail of the Double Church
of Two Faiths

9.42 Zollverein School of Management and Design
Architect: Sanaa

Active insulation

For the Zollverein School of Management and Design, architects Sanaa used an active approach to achieving insulation and thermal comfort. The school is the first building in the Office for Metropolitan Architecture's (OMA) masterplan for a disused mine in Essen, Germany. The external monolithic walls are formed of in situ concrete and are both internally and externally exposed. To 'insulate' the walls, Sanaa took advantage of the on-site excess pit water that has been pumped up from a depth of 1,000 m since the mine's closure in 1986 to avoid subsidence. The water emerges at a temperature of 29°C and was previously unused. The concrete walls utilise this free resource through an integrated polypropylene pipe system encased in the external walls, carefully spaced within the layer of reinforcing. The energy from the mine water is extracted by a heat exchange and then passed through a clean water circuit. The system can also work with cool water during the summertime for cooling. As a result, the walls have a thickness of 300 mm without the need for insulation. The system is designed to achieve a minimum temperature of 18°C on the inside of the wall. Should the pump system ever fail, the freezing of static water is prevented by a self-flushing system. Heat loss from the wall was expected

church is in situ concrete, which is 400 mm thick and fair-faced on both sides. The wall construction uses a lightweight aggregate to achieve a reasonable thermal performance without an insulative layer. In terms of energy consumption, the Double Church performs better than the contemporary Low Energy Building Standard of the city of Freiburg.

9.43 Zollverein School of Management and Design

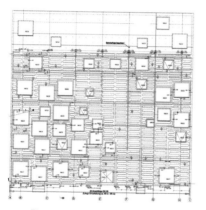

9.44 Elevation of the embedded pipe work

9.45 Internal elevation of the Zollverein
School of Management and Design

and the engineers, Transsolar Energietechnik, anticipated that a loss of 80% would still prove more economically viable than a double leaf construction. The Zollverein School is a provocative building, but the incorporation of insulation within the mix of the concrete, or as a declared layer, would seem to be a wise strategy that is applicable to a wider range of projects.

Thermal bridges – cold bridges

If a structural element or a component of a cladding system starts in a warm interior and is continuous to the outside, which may be very cold, then a thermal bridge or cold bridge has occurred or there is a loss of thermal partitioning. There are two primary risks if a cold bridge is allowed to occur in the construction: energy loss and the risk of condensation. First, dramatic thermal outflow resulting in significant heat and energy loss, negating the U-value and reducing the overall thermal performance of a building, and, second, the risk of a dew point forming within the construction and, thus, an increased risk of interstitial condensation. In 1983, Alan J. Brookes wrote in the first edition of *Cladding of Buildings*[9] that it was normal to find condensation on the back of precast concrete cladding. Over a generation later, this is now considered unacceptable, unless it is outside the weathering layer, as in a rain screen cladding system. Establishing the dew point for a given construction is a relatively easy calculation and *Thermal Insulation: Avoiding Risks* by C. Stirling[10] provides guidance on how to avoid such risks. Interstitial condensation can cause severe damage to the interior of a building and is sometimes mistaken for rain ingress. The sustained exposure to condensation can subject the internal finishes and paintwork to serious deterioration and mould growth, which is one of the major sources of respiratory allergies, such as asthma. Particular care needs to be taken when detailing concrete structures, as the high thermal mass of concrete can exacerbate the effect of a cold bridge.

There are a number of ways to avoid cold bridges, which involve the placement of the insulation and the avoidance of structural elements, such as a cantilever that passes through the insulation. If it is not always possible to avoid breaking through the insulative layer, there are now ranges of structural thermal breaks for use in concrete-to-concrete details and concrete-to-steel details – necessity has proven to be the 'mother' of invention. Schöck Isokorb's thermal broken structural subassemblies are examples of the options available. Structural thermal breaks are vital components and require detailed consideration for both the architect and the structural engineer.

Schöck Isokorb's structural thermal insulation assemblies provide structural continuity while minimising thermal flow. It integrates an insulating strip with a stainless steel re-bar to allow for sheer forces and a continuous bending moment through the slabs, while reducing the thermal conductivity between the elements. The high-density polystyrene units, at the core of this prefabricated component, contain high-density pressure-bearing blocks of micro stainless steel fibre-reinforced concrete. These blocks support a stainless steel re-bar that

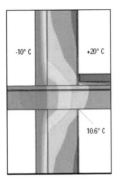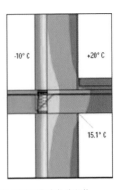

9.46 Thermal modelling of an external slab detail, showing the benefit of introducing a structural thermal break

9.47 Schöck thermal break for joining in situ concrete

accommodates shear and tension forces. The units are strong enough to transfer the loads, maintaining full structural integrity. Schöck weld stainless steel to mild steel reinforcement in order to protect against the risk of corrosion arising from any condensation that may occur within the thermal break; stainless steel also has the advantage of having a lower thermal conductivity than carbon steel. On each side of the thermal break, the reinforcement bars are lapped to provide structural continuity. Detailing around such junctions should accommodate the differential thermal movement between the construction elements, particularly when a range of materials is necessary to form the detail.

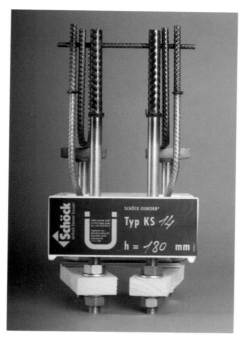

9.48 Steel to in situ concrete thermal break

9.49 Schöck Isokorb thermal breaks used as a hanging detail on the Lois Rosenthal Center for Contemporary Art

Lois Rosenthal Center for Contemporary Art

Schöck Isokorb provided thermal broken components for the hanging walls on the Lois Rosenthal Center for Contemporary Art in Cincinnati, designed by Zaha Hadid Architects, essential as the section of the gallery embraces internal and external spaces. The thermally broken Schöck Isokorb components are 1 m long and 400 mm high, and the insulated core is 80 mm thick.

The concrete industry is a resource that combines constructional technology, which has existed and been proven to be durable over millennia, with new techniques and material combinations that are continuously being developed. How you use concrete is your decision. To rework a famous saying by the furniture designer and architect Charles Eames – *the details are not details, they are the project.*

9.50 Lois Rosenthal Center for Contemporary Art
Designed by Zaha Hadid Architects

10.1 The atrium of Powergen Operational Headquarters
Architect: Bennetts Associates

TEN **sustainability**

'Our practice has delivered energy-efficient buildings in concrete for over twenty five years so we are in a good position to know that the theory works in practice, especially in a temperate climate such as the UK. By combining thermal mass and surface profile with good insulation and control over solar gain, building-types that are normally air-conditioned can achieve good working conditions through natural ventilation.'
Rab and Denise Bennetts[1]

Concrete has a very significant role to play in creating a sustainable and ecologically responsible built environment for humankind. It is a technology that dates back over two thousand years, and examples of concrete constructed by the Romans remain highly visited buildings in public use. The Pantheon in Rome is an excellent example of this (see Figure 8.4).

Although we should consider how to demolish new buildings at the end of their life as part of the initial design process, it is important that the construction industry is not drawn into a discussion about recycling as if buildings are just packaging. One of the keys to a sustainable built environment is the quality of the design embedded in the architecture or infrastructure. Frequently, well-designed buildings are reused rather than demolished after their first use is no longer required, thus saving the original embodied energy and the cultural value of the building. It is pertinent to note that Tate Modern, formerly a power station designed by Giles Gilbert Scott, is one of the most visited buildings in the south east of England. In 2005, Tate Modern was used by over 4.1 million people. Sir Nicolas Serota, the director of Tate Modern, noted that 'on the last day of the Olafur Eliasson exhibition in 2003 the gallery was busier than Bluewater',[2] which is Europe's largest shopping mall.

10.2 *Shibboleth* crossing the concrete floor of the Turbine Hall at Tate Modern
Artist: Doris Salcedo

When considering buildings and infrastructure that has reached the end of its first life, the order of decision-making should be: reuse of the building; reuse of the component; and finally recycling, if the other two options are not appropriate. The Gemini Residence, designed by MVRDV with JJW Architects, which was first occupied in 2005, is an excellent example of reuse and reinvention – two 25 m diameter concrete grain silos have been reused to form the courtyards of dockside apartments in Copenhagen. Christian Hanak and Eva Ørum, in *New Architecture in Copenhagen*, delight

10.3 The Gemini Residence inventively reuses two existing reinforced concrete grain silos
Designed by MVRDV with JJW Architects

10.4 Head of a new entrance doorways to the Gemini Residence, which has been precisely diamond cut out of the existing concrete cylinders, revealing the steel reinforcing bars

in this architectural act of reinvention: 'It was a stroke of genius to place the apartments outside the two concrete cylinders.'[3] The interiors of the former silos are now caped by diaphanous ethyl tetra fluoro ethylene (ETFE) pillows. They provide a generous semi-public space, giving access to the apartments.

When designing a new build project, architects need to consider two key environmental issues: how to reduce the carbon emissions associated with the running of a building; and how to reduce the carbon embodied in the construction of the project. This may include using alternatives to Portland cement, secondary or recycled aggregates, and offsite manufacturing. All of which will reduce the carbon footprint of the construction process and, as we make more energy efficient buildings, the embodied CO_2 of the building's fabric becomes a more significant factor. It is vital the quality of the spaces and the comfort of the occupants remain at the top of the agenda; in an office building, for example, the most expensive and the most valuable resource are the people using the building.

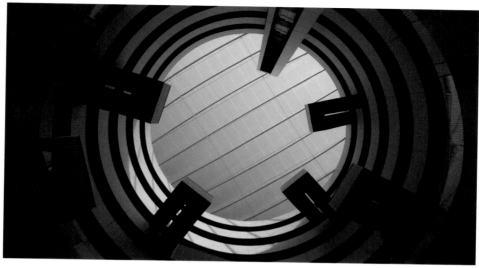

10.5 The concrete silos are now capped by pillows of ETFE

Lifecycle

Concrete that is well detailed and carefully constructed readily achieves a life expectancy of over 100 years. The normative first life of a road bridge in the UK is over 120 years. The concrete should require little maintenance, however, it is important that it is inspected annually and any problems that may occur should be repaired immediately.

Whole Life Costing (WLC) is a powerful tool designed to assist in assessing the cost and performance of construction – aimed at decision making, assisting in the choice between options that differ both in construction and operational costs over a defined time span. Capital costs, site adaptation and refurbishment, design fees and cost in use (including maintenance, cleaning, security, energy and insurances), rent/rates and other specific business facilities management services are also considered. Associated finance and income, taxation and residual value/disposal costs can also be included.

A key part of the WLC assessment also addresses environmental and sustainability aspects.

The application of WLC:

- encourages communication and project definition;
- clarifies the cost of ownership and occupation;
- optimises the total cost of ownership/occupation;
- ensures an early assessment of risks;
- promotes realistic budgeting;
- encourages discussion and decisions about material choices;
- ensures the best value is attained; and
- provides actual figures for future benchmarking.

It is important to not just consider the first cost of a proposed project, however the pressures to reduce the capital cost of project cannot just be ignored. A more responsible approach is to consider the WLC of a project, thinking beyond the capital cost by including energy running costs and embodied energy costs, over a time period or lifecycle agreed with the client. In 'Whole-Life Costs Concrete vs Steel', David Wright undertook a comparison of two identically dimensioned office buildings, one with a steel frame and, the second, an in situ concrete frame. [4] Although the steel-framed option has the lower capital cost by 3.6% over a 30-year period, the concrete-framed office building represents a saving of over 4%, this is predominately the result of the passive cooling achieved by the thermal mass of the concrete frame. As energy costs increase, this improvement and overall saving will grow to be even more significant, which should be considered alongside the 57 tonnes of CO_2 saved each year by using a concrete frame.

10.6 A plattenbauen that is about to be demolished

Life expectancy of a range of materials

When specifying a material for a particular task within a project, do architects consider the life expectancy of the material sufficiently? This can be influenced by the way a building is used and maintained. It is a good principle to inspect buildings and infrastructure annually, and to carry out any necessary preventative maintenance that may be required. This is much more cost-effective than neglecting the architecture and waiting for things to go wrong. Table 10.1 shows the typical life expectancy for a range of construction materials and is sourced from the *Guideline for Sustainable Building*.[5]

Another robust source on life expectancy figures is the *Life Expectancy of Building Components: A Practical Guide to Surveyors' Experiences of Buildings in Use*.[6]

Recycled precast concrete panels

Although concrete is capable of achieving a life expectancy of over one hundred years, it is not unusual for some buildings, if badly detailed, to age poorly or to outlive their original social era. This has been an issue with Government-commissioned tower blocks, originally designed to provide affordable housing. The demolition of an in situ cast tower block can provide a significant quantity of recycled aggregate, but, unlike timber and steel, it is not possible to carefully remove and preserve complete building components for reuse. However, if a tower block constructed of precast panels is demolished carefully, panels can be reclaimed and used again to build new forms of housing, saving the original embodied energy of the manufacture. Hervé Biele of architectural practice Conclus has deigned new housing in Mehrow, near Berlin, that reuses precast concrete panels from an unwanted 11-storey slab block or plattenbauen. The new houses cost 30% less because of the reuse of the precast concrete panels.

Table 10.1: Typical life expectancy for a range of construction materials

Element	Material	Life expectancy (years)	Average life expectancy (years)
Foundations	Concrete	80–150	100
Interior walls	Concrete	100–150	120
	Steel	80–100	90
	Softwood	50–80	70
	Hardwood	80–150	100
Stairs and balconies	Concrete	100–150	100
	Steel (internal)	80–100	90
	Steel (external)	50–90	60
	Softwood (internal)	50–80	60
	Hardwood (internal)	80–150	90
	Softwood (external)	30–50	45
	Hardwood (external)	50–80	70
Roof structures	Concrete	80–150	100
	Steel	60–100	70
	Timber	80–150	70
	Glued truss	40–80	50
	Nailed truss	30–50	30
Exterior facings	Concrete	100–150	120
	Softwood	40–50	45
	Hardwood	60–80	70
Boundary protection	Treated softwood	15–25	20
	Hardwood	25–35	30
	Galvanised/plastic coated metal	30–40	35
	Precast concrete	60–80	70

10.7 The recycled precast concrete panels

The architects reused intact precast concrete wall panels and floor plates from a demolished communist-era tower block (or plattenbauen). By doing this, the energy consumption that is usually associated with both concrete design and demolition was significantly reduced. Reusing concrete panels reduces the fuel costs that are usually associated with tower block demolition and the production of new concrete from the recycled aggregates. It can also be advantageous due to the fact that concrete hardens and increases in strength with age.

10.8 Mehrow Residence – interior during construction
Designed by Hervé Biele of Conclus

10.10 Mehrow Residence

10.9 Mehrow Residence – under construction

The only significant energy costs arise from the transportation of the 5 tonne panels and the use of a portable crane to lift them into place on site. However, the usual fuel emissions associated with aggregate extraction, cement manufacture and mixing are eliminated, making this a very environmentally friendly option. It is also very cost-effective. For the Mehrow Residence, the demolition firm provided the panels free of charge, which saved them the disposal cost and saved the architects the material cost. It can, however, be problematic to use recycled concrete panels on a small-scale scheme such as Conclus' Mehrow Residence. Although the panels are quick and simple to erect, their weight makes transportation and storage difficult, and they may need to be cut down to size. Timing is also an important issue for a scheme using recycled concrete panels, as there must be a demolition site close by and for transport to remain cost-effective, say within 100 miles. LEED in North America would apply a distance of 500 miles for the supply of components, reflecting the large-scale geography of that continent.[7] With the addition of 300 mm of insulation, double glazing and an appropriate heating system, a recycled concrete panel house can be up to three times more energy efficient than a normal house and, at approximately £521 per m², 30–40% cheaper than building a structural frame from scratch.

Reducing the embodied energy of concrete

The production of Portland cement requires a significant amount of energy. It is currently the most common form of cement, typically accounting for 10–15% of concrete by weight. In addition to the energy requirements of the 1,450°C furnace, CO_2 is produced from the chemical reaction when heating the calcium carbonate. However, over the past 40 years the energy consumption of cement has fallen by over 40%, from 7.5 GJ per tonne in 1962 to 4.5 GJ per tonne in 1997. Correspondingly, the embodied CO_2 (ECO_2) has also dropped. Direct CO_2 emissions related to the production of cement have been reduced by 29% between 1990 and 2006. The quantity of fossil fuels used to produce cement has been reduced by 29% since 1998 by the burning of waste-derived alternative fuels.[8]

Cement production in the UK accounts for 2% of the CO_2 emissions, compared with approximately 50% from the heating and lighting of buildings and 30% from transportation.

10.11 Inside a cement kiln

Alternatives to Portland cement

Embodied CO_2 can be reduced further by the use of an industrial by-product with cementitious properties, such as ground granulated blastfurnace slag (ggbs) and pulverised fuel ash (PFA), see Chapter 3. According to the Cementitious Slag Makers Association (founded in 1985), and based on research by the Building Research Establishment (BRE), each year in the UK more than two million tonnes of ggbs is used as cement.[9] By replacing the use of Portland cement, this annually:

- reduces CO_2 emissions by some two million tonnes;
- reduces primary energy use by 2,000 million kWh;
- saves three million tonnes of quarrying; and
- saves a potential landfill of two million tonnes.[10]

For more information on the specification of ggbs see BS EN 15167-1:2006 *ggbs*. The degree to which Portland cement can be substituted is dependent on factors such as the structural function of the concrete and its desired curing time. Table 10.3 compares the embodied CO_2 of various specifications of concrete, using mixes of Portland cement, PFA and ggbs.

Table 10.2: The embodied carbon dioxide (ECO_2) of concrete elements

Concrete	Concrete type	ECO_2 in $kgCO_2$ per m^3	ECO_2 in $kgCO_2$ per tonne
Blinding, mass fill, strip footings, mass foundations[a]	GEN1 70 mm (CEM I only)	173	75
Trench foundations[a]	GEN1 120 mm* (CEM I only)	184	80
Reinforced foundations[a]	RC30 70 mm‡ (CEM I only)	318	132
Ground floors[a]	RC35 70 mm† (CEM I only)	315	133
Structural: in situ floors, superstructure, walls, basements[a]	RC40 70 mm‡ (CEM I only)	372	153
High-strength concrete[a]	RC50 70mm‡ (CEM I only)	436	176
Dense concrete aggregate block[b]	Precast block	147	75
Aerated concrete block[b]	Precast block	121	240
Generic lightweight aggregate block[c]	Precast block	168	120
Timber			
Timber, UK sawn hardwood[d]		369	470
Timber, UK sawn softwood[d]		185	440
Plywood[d]		398	750
Steel			
UK produced structural steel sections[e]		15,313	1,932

* includes 25 kg/m^3 steel reinforcement
† includes 30 kg/m^3 steel reinforcement
‡ includes 100 kg/m^3 steel reinforcement

References:
a. The ECO_2 figures for GEN 1, RC32/40 and RC40/50 were derived using industry agreed representative figures for cementitious materials, aggregates, reinforcement, admixtures and an appropriate figure for water.
b. BRE Environmental Profiles database, Building Research Establishment (BRE), 2006.
c. Communication from the Environment Division, BREEAM Centre, Building Research Establishment (BRE), 2005.
d. Hammond, G. and Jones, C. (2006) *Inventory of Carbon & Energy (ICE) version 1.5 Beta*, Department of Mechanical Engineering, University of Bath.
e. Amato, A. and Eaton, K., J. (1998) *A Comparative Environmental Life Cycle Assessment of Modern Office Buildings*, Steel Construction Institute.

Table 10.3: The embodied carbon dioxide (ECO_2) of concrete mixes

Concrete	Concrete type	ECO_2 in $kgCO_2$ per tonne			ECO_2 in $kgCO_2$ per m³		
		CEM I concrete	30% fly ash concrete	50% ggbs concrete	CEM I concrete	30% fly ash concrete	50% ggbs concrete
Blinding, mass fill, strip footings, mass foundations[a]	GEN1 70 mm	173	124	98	75	54	43
Trench foundations[a]	GEN1 120 mm*	184	142	109	80	62	47
Reinforced foundations[a]	RC30 70 mm‡	318	266	201	132	110	84
Ground floors[a]	RC35 70 mm†	315	261	187	133	110	79
Structural: in situ floors, superstructure, walls, basements[a]	RC40 70 mm‡	372	317	236	153	131	97
High-strength concrete[a]	RC50 70 mm‡	436	356	275	176	145	112
Dense concrete aggregate block[b]	Precast block		147			75	
Aerated concrete block[b]	Precast block		121			240	
Lightweight aggregate block[c]	Precast block		168			120	

* includes 25 kg/m³ steel reinforcement
† includes 30 kg/m³ steel reinforcement
‡ includes 100 kg/m³ steel reinforcement

References:
a. The ECO_2 figures for GEN 1, RC32/40 and RC40/50 were derived using industry agreed representative figures for cementitious materials, aggregates, reinforcement, admixtures and an appropriate figure for water.
b. BRE Environmental Profiles database, Building Research Establishment (BRE), 2006.
c. Communication from the Environment Division, BREEAM Centre, Building Research Establishment (BRE), 2005.

Recycled steel reinforcement

All steel reinforcement produced in the UK is made from 100% recycled steel, which at the end of its life can be recovered and recycled again.[11] Recycled steel reinforcement also has a lower embodied energy compared with structural steel. When producing reinforcing steel, the energy consumption is fundamentally based on the energy used to melt and reform it. In contrast, structural steel manufacture in the UK is typically produced from iron ore, through an energy intensive process. As a result, the energy input per tonne of steel reinforcement is reduced by about half that for structural steel. The typical embodied energy of a steel rod is 24.6 MJ/kg and for recycled steel it is 11 MJ/kg.[12]

Two common forms of steel production are the basic oxygen and electric arc processes. In the electric arc process, 'cold' ferrous material, which is typically 100% scrap steel, is the major component, and is melted with alloys in an electric furnace. In the basic oxygen process, molten iron is removed from the blast furnace, combined with alloys, and up to 30% steel scrap is used as an additive to lower the temperature of the molten composition. In both processes, high-pressure oxygen is blown into the furnace, causing a chemical reaction that separates the molten steel and impurities, which can be removed as slag (see above for the production of ggbs).

Aggregate

The UK is fortunate in having an abundant supply of aggregates that can be extracted from numerous sites throughout the country, meaning that aggregate can often be sourced locally, minimising the impact of transportation. Typically, about 10% of the embodied energy of concrete is a result of transportation. For remote sites, transportation by water or rail will minimize CO_2 production. Central London still has quays where aggregates are brought in by ship up the River Thames and transported away by train.

It is also possible to use recycled aggregate to reduce the environmental impact of the concrete. The sources of recycled aggregate predominantly rely on the reuse of construction material and the use of waste material from industrial processes, which is known as secondary aggregate. Recycled aggregate is obtained from reprocessed, redundant construction materials such as tiles, bricks and concrete, or asphalt plannings from road maintenance works. It can be bought from demolition sites or specialist processing centres. It is more energy efficient if the aggregate is processed in situ at the demolition site, as this can significantly reduce transport costs and the environmental impact of excessive lorry movements. When construction works replace existing structures, the demolished structure can often be reused as the aggregate of sections of the new construction.

Technical requirements for the use of recycled aggregates in concrete

In comparison with gravel, recycled aggregates have divergent properties that require careful consideration when composing a proposed concrete mix. The limit values for contaminates within recycled aggregates are based on various strength and durability aspects, such as:

- the retarding influence on cement hardening;
- the corrosion of reinforcement (chlorides);
- swelling under the influence of moisture absorption (e.g. wood);
- the formation of ettringite (swelling caused by, e.g., gypsum);
- alkali–silica reactivity (e.g. Pyrex glass); and
- a decrease of compressive strength (e.g. asphalt).

Special attention needs to be paid to the drying shrinkage of concrete with recycled aggregates. For the determination of the chloride contents, the soluble value is recommended. Leaching limits are also proposed for the following

Table 10.4: Classification of recycled aggregates

Requirements	Type I	Type II	Type III	Test method
Minimum dry particle density (kg/m³)	1,500	2,000	2,400	BS EN 1097-6
Maximum weight % with SSD < 2,200 kg/m³	–	10	10	BS EN 1744-1 section 13.2 modified as ASTM C123
Maximum weight % with SSD < 1,800 kg/m³	10	1	1	
Maximum weight % with SSD < 1,000 kg/m³	1	0.5	0.5	
Maximum weight % of foreign materials (metals, glass, soft material, tar, crushed asphalt, etc.)	5	1	1	Test by visual separation as in BS EN 933-7

Note 1: BS EN 1744-1 section 12.2 separates material only at a density of 2,000 kg/m³;
BS EN 933-7 is a sorting method, but only for the determination of shell content.
Note 2: The water absorption test is not used to classify recycled aggregates. However, for the purpose of guidance only, the following values would be indicative of the various types of materials.

Table 10.5: Maximum water absorption value

For the purpose of guidance	Type I	Type II	Type III	Test method
Maximum water absorption value (weight %)	20	10	3	BS EN 1097-6

components: sugars, phosphate, nitrate, zinc, lead, sodium and potassium, determined with the tank-leaching test in accordance with BS EN 1744-1:2009. Table 10.4 presents a summary of the most important requirements.

Specifications are the same as natural aggregates with reference to size distribution, shape, alkali-aggregate reactions and the content of material, which can alter the range of the setting and hardening of the concrete. The content of fines is allowed to be up to 5%, while this fraction will normally not be composed of clay particles. The content of sulphur containing compounds is allowed to be 1%. Leaching and contamination is limited in accordance with national specifications.

Quality control
Density, impurities and water absorption are measured during production at least once a week. Impact control and general description (type) are determined for every delivery. The density grading is controlled at least two times per year.

Secondary aggregates
These are usually by-products of other industrial processes, which are not necessarily associated with the construction industry. Depending on their origin, these by-products can be further defined as manufactured or natural. Manufactured secondary aggregates include slag from iron and steel manufacture and ash from the bottom of coal-fired power station incinerators, while typical naturally occurring secondary aggregates include slate waste and stent from china clay production. Separated from the china clay by high-pressure hoses,

10.12 Stent at Bardon Aggregates' Littlejohn Quarry near St Austell

stent is granite rock that is usually treated as waste. Typically, 4.5 tonnes of stent is produced for every tonne of china clay. Stockpiles of material make secondary aggregates readily available to the construction industry.

Using secondary materials may result in the concrete having a strong regional characteristic. For instance, in the UK, secondary aggregate might predominantly consist of china clay sand in the South West of England and metallurgical slag in South Wales, Yorkshire and Humberside.

10.13 Number 1 Coleman Street
Designed by Swanke Hayden Connell Architects
with David Walker Architects

For the concrete main frame of Number 1 Coleman Street, an office development in the City of London for Stanhope, built during 2006 and designed by Swanke Hayden Connell Architects with David Walker Architects, the engineers Arup specified 1,005 tonnes of secondary aggregate in the form of stent. This project represents the first major use of stent outside the South West of England. Bryan Marsh of Arup noted that: 'By virtue of the secondary aggregate and alternative cementitious material [PFA], the overall recycled/secondary content of the concrete increased tenfold from the 5% level typical of current construction to 50% by mass and from 15% to approximately 45% by value. When the reinforcement was included this rose to approximately 77% by value.'[13]

Thinness

The cost of materials and the energy required to produce them places a key constraint on all designers and architects to use as little of a material as possible to deliver a durable and effective component. The minimal use of materials, including concrete, is directly linked to sustainability. The use of high-performance concrete for structural components is reviewed in Chapter 2, and Chapter 6 sets out strategies for achieving economical long spans. One technique for reducing the quantity of concrete required for a slab, and thus its self-weight, is by forming voids. Proprietary systems, such as Bubble Deck and Cobiax, offer complete floor slab systems to minimise concrete usage. In this technique, recycled plastic spheres are trapped between two layers of reinforcing mesh, forming a two-way spanning hollow slab. It should be noted that the use of void formers limits the potential for integrating services into the slab and that this should be considered at the design stage; incorporating waterborne heating and cooling pipe work is not a problem, however, recessed light fittings can be problematic or require careful coordination to avoid the void formers.

10.14 Bubble deck – recycled plastic spheres minimise the concrete required to form the structural slab

10.15 Levelling the concrete on a bubble deck slab

10.16 New Laboratories of Expertex Textile Centrum – note the surface-mounted light fittings
Architect: Brookes Stacey Randall with IAA Architecten

Environmental responsibility

The cement and concrete industries have demonstrated a strong commitment to environmental responsibility and seek to continuously improve its performance. All cement works in the UK are certified to ISO 140001: 2004, *Environmental Management Systems* as a minimum. The Concrete Industry Alliance *Environmental Report*,[14] produced in 2000, notes the commitment of the cement and concrete industry to continuous environmental improvement. From 1994–98 the following improvements were made (per unit weight of concrete):

- 2% less carbon dioxide;
- 48% less sulphur dioxide;
- 14% less nitrogen dioxide; and
- 24% less particulate emissions.

Between 1998 and 2006 the following further improvements were made:

- 29% less carbon dioxide (combined value 1990 to 2006);
- 46% less sulphur dioxide;
- 17% less nitrogen dioxide; and
- 60% less particulate emissions.

The Concrete Industry continues to seek further improvements to improve its economic viability and reduce its overall environmental impact. In 2008, the Concrete Industry in the UK published a strategy aimed at becoming leaders in sustainable construction and, in 2009, they published its first annual sustainable performance review, as part of its commitment to continuous improvement.[15]

The importance of thermal mass

Materials with a high thermal mass are capable of slowly accumulating, and slowly releasing, thermal energy. High thermal mass is a consequence of a high density, high specific heat capacity and a relatively low thermal conductivity – materials such as earth, stone,

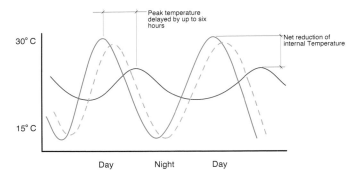

10.17 Fabric energy storage created by exposed thermal mass

water and concrete. Utilising the thermal mass of building materials is known as fabric energy storage.

Fabric energy storage can be employed to regulate temperatures within a building, minimising the need for energy-consuming systems such as air-conditioning. Heat is absorbed from the sun, as well as incidental gains from people, artificial lighting and electrical equipment. Internally exposed concrete will absorb these gains, until it is balanced with the internal temperature, and will then release the energy when the internal temperature drops – creating a lag and a reduction in peak temperature. The amount of energy it can store, and the period of this lag time, is proportional to its mass and its exposure. For fabric energy storage to operate effectively, a strategy for absorbing and releasing the accumulated energy must be employed, or the structure will simply stay averagely warm during the summer, and averagely cold during the winter. Ideally, a lag time of 12 hours will offset and reduce the peak temperature by the maximum value. Another possibility is to utilise a seasonal, six-month lag-time, though this requires a very high mass and will usually rely upon ground temperatures, as in earth shelter construction.

Fabric energy storage can be controlled by either passive or active cooling methods. Natural ventilation is the most basic method, but is dependent on lower night-time external temperatures. Passive systems are suitable for gains of up to 30 W/m², where natural ventilation can be used. Single-sided natural ventilation will operate at a plan depth of up to twice the floor to ceiling height, while cross-ventilation operates at depths of five times the floor to ceiling height. Active systems allow for higher performance, and improved control, as well as the potential for heat recovery from the ventilation. Passing water through the concrete, in connection with a ground storage tank, or heat exchanger, increases the effective thermal mass, and can potentially be combined with a heating system. Thermal mass and insulation perform different, often complementary, functions and should not be confused. Due to their density, a material of high thermal mass will usually have a poor insulating ability, while a highly insulating material will have a low thermal mass. Insulation blocks the passage of thermal energy; thermal mass absorbs it.

Embodied energy, although significant in the selection of a building material, represents a relatively small investment when compared with the energy used by a typical late twentieth-century building. For example, in a four to six storey building, with a life expectancy of

60 years, the production of the building fabric only accounts for 10% of the environmental impact. The other 90% of environmental impact is from the heating, cooling and lighting of the building. This can be transformed by the use of a high standard of insulation, combined with the aid of thermal mass and a building design that allows for efficient daylighting and controlled solar gain. For buildings designed to use a low amount of energy at low running costs, the embodied energy of construction becomes a more significant factor and should influence the architect's design decisions. In a comparison of concrete and steel structures, the embodied energy of a concrete frame will be, on average, 1.5 to 2.5 GJ/m^2 compared with 2.6 to 2.9 GJ/m^2 for structural steel.[16]

10.18 Inland Revenue Building, Nottingham
Architect: Michael Hopkins Architects

For concrete to absorb thermal energy efficiently, the internal surface of the concrete floor slab, wall or column must be exposed to the interior of the building, rather than be concealed by a ceiling or cladding material. This provides architects with aesthetic opportunities that relate directly to the holistic performance of the architecture. The shape and finish of a concrete slab can be manipulated to create maximum thermal absorption by increasing its surface area, while facilitating natural light and incorporating artificial lighting. It is essential that the soffit remains exposed – there always should be a line of sight of the soffit for all occupants.

An exposed soffit can be painted, typically in a light colour, to allow light to be reflected into the building. This will reduce the need for artificial lighting by making the daylight more effective. An inherently light colour can be achieved by the use of white cement or ggbs. In some cases, such as the Inland Revenue Building in Nottingham by Michael Hopkins Architects, the decision was made to paint the concrete with a mineral paint to achieve consistent light reflectance for the daylight and up lighting. The finish of an exposed concrete surface is determined by the mix, formwork used and mode of production (see Chapters 2 and 3).

The Powergen Operational Headquarters building, designed by Bennetts Associates and completed in 1994, was one of the first office buildings in the UK to use an internally exposed concrete structure to provide thermal mass (see Figure 10.1). Night-time cooling is provided by the windows, electronically operated by a building management system. One of the advantages of this approach is that the concrete must remain exposed – it is the interior architecture of the project, thus minimising the risks of a secondary layer of interior design being added by the client or incoming tenant. During his 2003 Lubetkin lecture, Rab Bennetts noted that working with concrete to build low-energy buildings that had high-quality interiors 'offered the chance to re-establish some architectural authenticity in the office as a building-type'[17] (see Chapter 3 for details of the onsite precasting of the floor slabs of the Powergen building). The concrete soffit has a curved boat-like profile, which integrates services and lighting. Bennetts observed: 'The concrete coffers became the symbol of the project – a synthesis of engineering, economy, construction

10.19 The Informatics Forum of the Potterrow
Development for the University of Edinburgh
uses the exposed thermal mass of the concrete
frame, walls and soffit (2008)
Architect: Bennetts Associates

and, above all, architectural space.'[18] Wessex
Water, also by Bennetts Associates, uses a
similar environmental strategy and achieved
an Excellent Environmental Assessment
Award under BREEAM 98 for Offices from
the Building Research Establishment (BRE),
and has been extensively evaluated after
occupation. The use of internally exposed
concrete allows the architect a way of unifying
performance and aesthetics.

The most valuable assets in any building
are the people. A knowledge-based economy
only serves to emphasise this point. In the
twenty-first century, collectively, we should
be designing architecture that is comfortable
and enjoyable to work in by creating humane
architecture that facilitates interaction. The
Potterrow Development, designed by Bennetts
Associates for the University of Edinburgh,

is an exemplar of this approach, providing
a timely and vital contrast to the form-
derived buildings that seem to dominate the
architectural publications today.

The Potterrow Development, completed in 2008,
has a simple in situ concrete frame with flat
slabs, which typically span 6.5 m or 7.5 m,
except over the ground-floor meeting rooms
where down stands and post-tensioning were
introduced to achieve a 13 m clear span. The
shear walls and concrete soffits are exposed
throughout to provide thermal mass; a vital
component in the low-energy strategy for this
intensively used building, providing a thermal
flywheel that facilitates night cooling. Some
academics can have up to eight computers in
their rooms. Therefore, mechanical ventilation
with heat reclaim is provided, with air being
drawn into the atrium and exhausted at a
high level, thus benefiting from the stack
effect. The staff and students have the option
of opening windows for natural ventilation
in their offices. The exposed concrete soffits
have been painted with vibrant colours based
on Eduardo Paolozzi's *Turing Prints*. These
are particularly striking in the two-storey
mini-forums that form key day-to-day meeting
spaces for the staff. The soffit generates soft
glowing coloured daylight that spills out into
the adjacent spaces. For the cladding details of
the Potterrow Development, see Chapter 9.

The Informatics Forum is an excellent higher
education building that benefits from Bennetts
Associates' experience of designing cost-
effective low-energy and high-quality office
headquarters over the past 20 years. This is
flexible, durable and humane architecture. Only
the spaces of Herzberg's Centraal Beheer in
Apledoorn rival the relaxed social spaces that
surround this Forum.

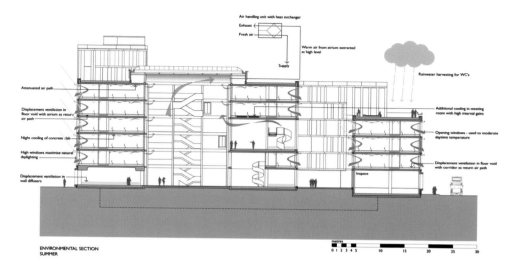

10.20 Section through the Informatics Forum of the University of Edinburgh
– summer ventilation strategy

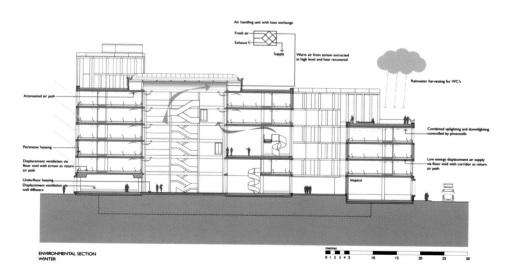

10.21 Section through the Informatics Forum of the University of Edinburgh
– winter ventilation strategy

Cool running in California

The United States Federal Building in San Francisco, California, is one of the first major office buildings in the US to be naturally ventilated for over 70 years. Above the fifth floor, this office building, designed by Morphosis for the General Services Administration (GSA), is naturally ventilated, providing high-quality workspaces that require only modest quantities of primary energy to

10.22 Northwest elevation of the United States Federal Building, San Francisco, California

Architect: Morphosis with engineers Ove Arup and Partners

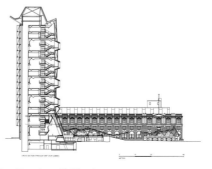

10.23 Key sections of the United States Federal Building, San Francisco, California

10.24 The Skycourt of the United States Federal Building, San Francisco, California

this project represents the epitome of an optimistic architecture; an architecture that synthesizes its complex forces and realities into a coherent whole.'[19]

The Federal Building uses only 45% energy consumption of a typical GSA office and is being monitored by the GSA Energy Centre. This reduction in energy demand is primarily the result of three environmental strategies that are fully integrated into the architecture of this office building: the maximisation of daylight and the control of solar gain combined with natural ventilation that is computer controlled. The naturally ventilated floors only use 86.9 kWh of electricity per m² per year. Lighting is typically the largest energy requirement of an office building. The United States Federal Building incorporates a slender tower that is 18 storeys high, but

10.25 Key plans of the United States Federal Building, San Francisco, California

create comfortable conditions. The exposed internal concrete structure is a vital component in achieving comfort because it provides accessible thermal mass that can store energy on a diurnal basis. Thom Mayne, the founder of Morphosis, writing about the design of this project, observes:

'When architecture engages social, cultural, political, and ethic currents, it has the potential to transform the world and our place in it. For me,

only 19.8 m wide to facilitate daylighting and cross-ventilation. This in conjunction with a generous floor to ceiling height of over 3.25 m, which enables 85% of the workplace to be day lit. The offices also afford its occupants excellent views across San Francisco. It is highly appropriate for GSA to pioneer a low-energy office building as it administers all of the federal government buildings in the USA. High-performance façades are vital in achieving this energy saving, while creating pleasant workspaces.

10.26 A typical office in the United States Federal Building, San Francisco, California – possibly showing that there is too much solar gain entering via the double façade

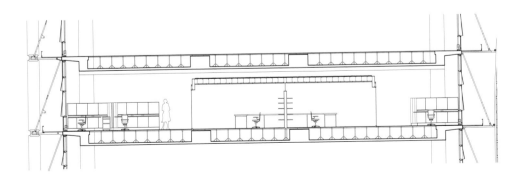

10.27 Typical office floor section of the United States Federal Building, San Francisco, California

10.28 The exposed waveform concrete soffit of the United States Federal Building

The south-eastern elevation of the tower is protected from excessive solar gains by perforated stainless steel sunscreens. A double façade of fixed translucent glass louvers, with an inner layer of openable double glazed windows, forms the north-eastern elevation. The public architecture of the tower is generated by these climate-specific façades.

The offices have waveform exposed concrete soffits providing thermal mass. The concrete is cooled at night by automated opening vents that are controlled by a building management system. In its use of exposed concrete to define the interior and to provide thermal mass, this building has clear antecedence with the Powergen Operational Headquarters building in Warwickshire, by Bennetts Associates, and the Inland Revenue building in Nottingham,

by Hopkins Architects. Thus, it is no surprise to find that the structural engineers were Ove Arup & Partners. The creamy coloured concrete of the soffit is a result of using ggbs in the mix; it replaced 50% of the Portland cement. The saving in embodied CO_2 normally associated with the use of ggbs, an industrial by-product of iron production, was limited in this case as the ggbs was sourced from Korea.

In the twenty-first century, humankind has the benefit of a millennia of construction technology that can be combined with digital design and the digital modelling of performance. Collectively, we have the means to make altogether better architecture that serves our diverse cultures and helps to sustain planet earth. Concrete, an ancient yet radical material, has a vital role in sustaining human ecology.

notes

plasticity

1   Zaha Hadid quoted by Jonathan Glancey in 'I don't do nice', *The Guardian*, 9 October 2006, p. 21.
2   Yvenes, M. and Madshus, E. (eds) (2008) *Architect Sverre Fehn: Intuition, Reflection, Construction*, The National Museum of Art, Architecture and Design, Oslo, pp. 122–123.
3   For more information on Castlevecchio and the work of Carlo Scarpa, see Richard Murphy (1990) *Carlo Scarpa and Castlevecchio*, Butterworth Architecture.
4   Le Corbusier (1987) *The Decorative Arts of Today*, MIT Press, p195, translated by James Dunnett.

mix

1   Richard S. Wurman (1986) *What Will Be Has Always Been. The Words of Louis I Kahn*, Rizzoli, p. 152.
2   In accordance with ISO 14688.
3   Yvenes, M. and Madshus, E. (eds) (2008) *Architect Sevrre Fehn: Intuition, Reflection, Construction*, The National Museum of Art, Architecture and Design, Oslo, p. 46.
4   David Bennett (2007) *Architectural Insitu Concrete*, RIBA Publications.
5   Concrete Industry (2009) *Sustainability Performance Report*, MPA.
6   David Bennett (September 2003) *Concrete Quarterly*, 205, pp. 10–13.
7   Paul Scott via email 2006.

in situ + precast

1   Tadao Ando interviewed in *Concrete Quarterly*, 217, Autumn 2006, p. 6.
2   Ian Lambot (1985) *The Construction: The New Headquarters for the HongKong and Shanghai Banking Corporation*, Dragages et Travaux Publics.
3   Rupasinghe R. and Nolan É. (2007) *Formwork for Modern, Efficient Concrete Construction*, BRE Press.
4   ibid.
5   Paul Scott via email 2006.
6   Thomas W. Leslie (2003) Form as Diagram of Forces: The Equiangular Spiral in the Work of Pier Luigi Nervi, *Journal of Architectural Education*, 57(2), pp. 45–54.
7   Concrete Industry (2009) *Sustainability Performance Report*, MPA.
8   Nikolaus Hirsh's comments recorded in David Bennett (2005) *The Art of Precast Concrete*, Birkhäuser, p. 114.
9   Goodchild, C. H. and Glass, J. (2004) *Best Practice Guidance for Hybrid Concrete Construction*, Concrete Centre. Note the DTI was replaced by the Department for Business, Enterprise and Regulatory Reform and the Department for Innovation, Universities and Skills in June 2007.
10 Michael Stacey was the partner in charge of Ballingdon Bridge at Brookes Stacey Randall Architects.
11 Michael Stacey (2007) *Searching For Excellence: Ballingdon Bridge*, ARQ, Vol.11, No.3/4, Cambridge University Press, pp 210–222.
12 Michael Stacey (July/August 2005) In My Craft and Sullen Art, *AD Special Edition: Design Through Making* (edited by Bob Sheil), Wiley, pp. 38–47.

formwork + finishes

1   Andrea Deplazes (ed.) (2005) *Constructing Architecture*, Birkhäuser, p. 57.
2   Based on a typology from Pfeifer, G., Liebers, A. M. and Brauneck, P. (2005) *Exposed Concrete: Technology and Design*, Birkhäuser.
3   CONSTRUCT (2010) *The National Structural Concrete Specification (NSCS)*, Concrete Structures Group.
4   Andre Bartak and Mike Shears (1972) The Emley Moor Television Tower, *The Structural Engineer*.
5   Helen Elias (2005) Fast-track new-build gets tunnel vision, *Concrete Quarterly*, 211 (spring) pp. 4–6.
6   Alan Chandler and Remo Predreschi (eds) (2007) *Fabric Formwork*, RIBA Publications.
7   Daniel Rosbottom quoted by Helen Elias (2005) The haphazard history of intervention was instrumental in dictating the approach of the architects, *Concrete Quarterly*, 214 (Winter).
8   Author's interview of Alan Jones, Belfast, 2006.
9   Peter Guillery (1993) The Buildings of London Zoo, *London Zoo*, p. 43.
10 Canply state: 'MDO plywood for concrete formwork provides a superior concrete finish with a smoother, whiter, matte-finish that resists grain and patch transfer. Harder, denser concrete surface resulting from a constant water/cement ratio maintained by the overlay's low water transmission rate. Depending on conditions of use, MDO panels are 20% to 40% stronger than standard Douglas Fir panels of the same thickness.' www.canply.org/english/products/overlaidplywood.htm (accessed in August 2009).
11 Graham Bizley (2009) Quirky detailing and a clever use of poured concrete give this new community centre a dramatic impact, *Concrete Quarterly*, 228 (Summer).
12 Adam Caruso quoted by Kieran Long (2009) Arts & Crafts, *Architects Journal*, 12.11.09, p. 29.

foundations

1   David Bennett (ed.) (2006) 04 Residential Delights, in *Concrete Elegance One*, Concrete Centre with RIBA Publications, p. 21.

2 At times it appears that the idea of structuring a work is more clearly understood by other disciplines, be it the organisation of a scientific investigation or the structure of a novel or an essay. This particularly applies to the contemporary teaching of architecture.

3 Sourced from Brookers, O. (2006) *Concrete Buildings Scheme Design Manual*, Concrete Centre.

4 Ibid.

5 Ibid.

6 Ibid.

7 Alan M. Jones (2006) Placing low energy architecture in a low cost economy, *Proceedings of PLEA2006 – the 23rd Conference on Passive and Low Energy Architecture*, Geneva, Switzerland, 6–8 September 2006.

8 Tony Butcher (2007) *Ground Source Heat Pumps*, IHSBREE Press for the NHBC Foundation.

9 Dunster, B., Simmons, C. and Gilbert, B. (2008) *The ZEDbook*, Taylor & Francis.

10 Butcher, A. P., Powell, J. J. M. and Skinner, H. D. (2006) *Reuse of Foundations in Urban Sites*, BRE Press.

11 For more details of this project see Colin Davies (1993) *Hopkins 1: The Work of Michael Hopkins and Partners*, Phaidon.

frames

1 Le Corbusier (1926) *Five Points of Modern Architecture*, Almanach de l'Architecture Moderne, Paris. Reprint of the 1926 edn published by G. Crès, Paris, in series *Collection de L'Esprit nouveau* (1975), Bottega D'Erasmo, Turin.

2 Goodchild C. H., Webster R. M. and Elliott K. S. (2009) *Economic Concrete Elements to Eurocode 2*, Concrete Centre.

3 Nikolaus Pevsner (1951) *The Buildings of England*, Penguin (second edn revised by Elizabeth Williamson (2003) Yale University Press), p. 70.

4 Ibid.

5 For more information on this project see David Cottam, (1986) *Sir Owen Williams 1890–1969*, Architectural Association, pp. 71–83.

6 Goodchild, C. H. *et al.* (2009) op. cit.

walls + blockwork

1 Frank Lloyd Wright (1932) *An Autobiography*, Pomegranate Communications (2005 edn), p.

2 Susan Dawson (2003) Ipswich Town on the ball with new stand, *Concrete Quarterly,* 206 (Winter), pp. 8–12.

3 Arnulf Lüchinger (1987) *Herman Hertzberger: Buildings and Projects*, Arch-Edition, p. 87.

4 Robust Details Ltd (2009) *Robust Details Handbook Edition 3*, Robust Details Limited.

5 Sean Smith (2010) *How to Achieve Acoustic Performance in Masonry Homes*, Concrete Centre.

6 Robust Details Ltd (2009) op. cit.

thinness + form

1 Fred Angerer (1960) *Surface Structures in Building, Alec Tiranti* (English edn translated by W. Redlich), p. 1.

2 Franz Hart (1951) H*ochbaukonstrktion für Architekten* – quoted in English by Angerer (1960) ibid., pp. 3–4.

3 Kenneth Frampton (1995) *Studies in Tectonic Culture: The Poetics of Construction in Nineteenth and Twentieth Century Architecture: Studies in Tectonic Culture*, MIT Press, pp. 267–268 (2001 edn).

4 Ibid., p. 273.

5 Ibid., p. 273.

6 Ibid., p. 278.

7 Ibid.

8 Ibid., pp. 281–283.

9 Román A. (2002) *Eero Saarinen: An Architecture of Multiplicity*, Laurence King, p. 191.

10 Kenneth Frampton (1995) op. cit., p. 273.

11 Jørn Utzon in conversation with Torsten Bløndal from Jørn Utzon (2005) *Log Book Volume 11*, Bagsvaerd Church, Edition Bløndal.

12 Kenneth Frampton (1995) op. cit., p. 292.

13 Jørn Utzon in conversation with Torsten Bløndal from Jørn Utzon (2005) *Log Book Volume 11*, Bagsvaerd Church, Edition Bløndal.

14 Ibid.

15 Quotation attributed to Richard Rogers, see Barbie Campbell Cole and Ruth Elias Rogers (eds) (1985) *Richard Rogers + Architects, Architectural Monographs*, p. 78; copyright Richard Rogers & Partners.

detail

1 Tadao Ando (2006) interviewed in *Concrete Quarterly*, (Autumn), p. 7.

2 The scientific evidence for climate change created by human industry is evident, the Intergovernmental Panel on Climate Change *Fourth Assessment Report* (AR4) states 'Warming of the climate system is unequivocal, as is now evident from observations of increases in global average air and ocean temperatures, widespread melting of snow and ice and rising global average sea level.' Intergovernmental Panel on Climate Change, *Fourth Assessment Report (AR4), Synthesis Report*, p. 30.

3 Approved Document L1A (2010) NDS, p. 16.

4 The Concrete Centre (2008) *Energy and CO_2: Achieving Targets with Concrete and Masonry*, The Concrete Centre.

5   Mario Cucinella interviewed by the author in Nottingham, 2008.

6   For further information on the School in Paspels by Architect Valerio Olgiati see Deplazes, Andrea (ed.) (2005) *Constructing Architecture: Materials Processes Structures: A Handbook*, Birkhäuser, pp. 332–340.

6   Rollo, J. (ed.) (2005) Double Church of Two Faiths, *C+A*, Issue 1, Australia, p. 15.

7   ibid.

8   Alan J. Brookes (1983) *Cladding of Buildings*, Construction Press.

9   C. Stirling (2002) *Thermal Insulation: Avoiding Risks*, British Research Establishment.

sustainability

1   Rab and Denise Bennetts via email to the author, 2008.

2   Jonathan Glancey (2006) Tate Modern 2: The Epic Sequel, *The Guardian*, 26 July 2006.

3   Christian Hanak and Eva Ørum (eds) (2008) *New Architecture in Copenhagen*, Danish Architecture Centre.

4   David Wright (2009) Whole-Life Costs Concrete vs Steel, *Building Magazine*, 23 June 2009 (available as a reprint/pdf from www.concretecentre.com).

5   German Federal Ministry of Transport, Building and Housing (2001) *Guideline for Sustainable Building, Federal Office for Building and Regional Planning*, edited from pp. 6.11–6.18.

6   Building Cost Information Service (2006) *Life Expectancy of Building Components: A Practical Guide to Surveyors' Experiences of Buildings in Use*, 2nd edn, Building Cost Information Service.

7   Leadership in Energy and Environmental Design (LEED) is run by the US Green Building Council, see www.usgbc.org.

8   Mike Gilbert (2007) *BCA Performance*, British Cement Association.

9   Dr Denis Higgins (2006), *Sustainable Concrete: How Can Additions Contribute?*, The Institute of Concrete Technology, Annual Technical Symposium, 28 March 2006.

10 Ibid.

11 Glass, J. (2001) *Ecoconcrete: The Contribution of Cement and Concrete to a More Sustainable Built Environment*, British Cement Association, p. 17.

12 Hammond, G. and Jones, C. (2006) *Inventory of Carbon & Energy (ICE) version 1.6a*, Department of Mechanical Engineering, University of Bath.

13 Bryan Marsh (2006) Arup trailblazes recycled material, *Concrete Quarterly*, 217, (Autumn), pp. 4–5.

14 Concrete Industry Alliance (2000) *Environmental Report for the UK Concrete Industry 1994–1998*, Concrete Industry Alliance.

15 The Concrete Industry (2009) *Sustainable Performance: 1st Report*, The Concrete Centre.

16 Glass, J. (2001) *Ecoconcrete: The Contribution of Cement and Concrete to a More Sustainable Built Environment*, British Cement Association, p. 13.

17 Rab Bennetts *Bennetts Associates Architects*, Lubetkin Lecture, October 2003, unpublished pdf of this lecture supplied by Rab Bennetts.

18 Ibid.

19 Personal communication: email to the author dated 25 November 2008 from Morphosis, Santa Monica, California.

further reading

Abel, Chris (1991) *Architecture In Detail: Renault Centre*, Phiadon.

Ando, Tadao (ed. Francesco Dal Co) (1998) *Tadao Ando: Complete Works*, Phaidon.

Angerer, Fred (1961) *Surface Structures In Building: Structure and Form*, Alec Tiranti Ltd.

Atelier Kinold Office (2000/01) *Building in Concrete*, München, Atelier Kinold.

Austin, C. K. (1960; 3rd edn 1978) *Formwork to Concrete*, Macmillan and Co. Ltd.

Bartak, Andre and Shears, Mike (1972) The Emley Moor Television Tower, *The Structural Engineer*, February.

Bechtold, Martin (2008) *Innovative Surface Structure: Technologies and Applications*, Taylor & Francis.

Bennett, David (2005) *The Art of Precast Concrete*, Basel, Birkhäuser.

Bennett, David (ed.) (2006) *Concrete Elegance One*, Concrete Centre with RIBA Publications.

Bennett, David (ed.) (2006) *Concrete Elegance Two*, Concrete Centre with RIBA Publications.

Bennett, David (ed.) (2007) *Concrete Elegance Three*, Concrete Centre with RIBA Publications.

Bennett, David (2007) *Architectural Insitu Concrete*, RIBA Publications.

Bennett, David (2009) *Concrete Elegance Four*, Concrete Centre with RIBA Publications.

Brookes, Alan J. (1973; 6th edn 2000) *Cladding of Building*, Spon.

Brooker, O. (2006) *Concrete Buildings Scheme Design Manual*, Concrete Centre.

Butcher, Tony (2007) *Ground Source Heat Pumps*, IHSBREE Press for NHBC Foundation.

Chandler, Alan and Predreschi, Remo (ed.) (2007) *Fabric Formwork*, RIBA Publications.

Cook, Peter (1985) Richard Rogers + Architects, Academy Editions.

Dawson, Susan (2003) *Cast In Concrete (A Guide to Precast Concrete and Reconstructed Stone)*, The Architectural Cladding Association.

Deplazes, Andrea (ed.) (2005) *Constructing Architecture: Materials Processes Structures: A Handbook*, Birkhäuser.

Dernie, David (2003) *New Stone Architecture*, Laurence King.

Dunster, Bill, Simmons, Craig and Gilbert, Bobby (2008) *The ZEDbook*, Taylor & Francis.

Everett, Alan and Baritt, C. H. M. (1994) *Mitchell's Materials*, Longman Group UK Ltd.

Faber, John and Alsop, David (1976; 6th edn 1979) *Reinforced Concrete Simply Explained*, Oxford University Press.

Ford, Edward, R. (1990) *The Details of Modern Architecture*, MIT Press.

Ford, Edward, R. (1996) *The Details of Modern Architecture, Volume. 2: 1928–1988*, MIT Press.

Foster, Jack Stroud (1973; 6th edn 2000) *Mitchell's Structure and Fabric Part 1*, Longman Group Ltd.

Frampton, Kenneth (1995) *Studies in Tectonic Culture: The Poetics of Construction in Nineteenth and Twentieth Century Architecture*, MIT Press.

Gilbert, Mike (2007) *BCA Performance 2007*, British Cement Association.

Goodchild, C. H. and Glass, Jacqueline (2004) *Best Practice Guidance for Hybrid Concrete Construction*, Concrete Centre.

Goodchild, C. H., Webster, R. M. and Elliott, K. S. (2009) *Economic Concrete Elements to Eurocode 2*, Concrete Centre.

Glass, Jacqueline (2001) *Ecoconcrete: The Contribution of Cement and Concrete to a More Sustainable Built Environment*, British Cement Association.

Gordon, J. E. (1978) *Structures: or Why Things Don't Fall Down*, Penguin Books Ltd.

Groàk, Steven (1992) *The Idea of Building*, Spon.

Guillery, Peter (1993) *The Buildings of London Zoo*, London Zoo.

Hammond, G. and Jones, C. (2006) *Inventory of Carbon and Energy (ICE) version 1.6a*, Department of Mechanical Engineering, University of Bath.

Hanak, Christian and Ørum, Eva (eds) (2008) *New Architecture in Copenhagen*, Danish Architecture Centre.

Hawkes, Dean (2006) *The Environmental Imagination*, Taylor and Francis.

Huxtable, Ada Louise (1960) *Masters of World Architecture*, Fredrick A. Praeger.

Kind-Barkauskas, Friendbert, Kauhsen, Bruno, Polónyi, Stefan and Brandt, Jörg (2002) *Concrete Consruction Manual*, Birkhäuser.

Lambot, Ian (1985) *The Construction: The New Headquarters for the HongKong and Shanghai Banking Corporation*, Dragages et Travaux Publics.

Lancaster, Lynne C. (2005) *Concrete Vaulter Construction In Imperial Rome*, Cambridge University Press.

Leslie, Thomas W. (2003) Form as Diagram of Forces: The Equiangular Spiral in the Work of Pier Luigi Nervi, *Journal of Architectural Education*.

Lipman, Jonathan (1986) *Frank Lloyd Wright and the Johnson Wax Building*, Rizzoli.

Littlefield, D. (2006) Thin Floors Create Roomy, Flexible Offices, *Concrete Quarterly*, 217, Autumn.

Lüchinger, Arnulf, (1987) *Herman Hertzberger: Buildings and Projects*, Arch-Edition.

MacDonald, William L. (1976) *The Pantheon: Design, Meaning and Progeny*, Penguin Books Ltd.

Melet, Ed (2002) *The Architectural Detail*, NAi Publishers.

Murphy, Richard (1990) *Carlo Scarpa and Castlevecchio*, Butterworth Architecture.

Ohno, Taiichi (1988) *Toyota Production System: Beyond Large-Scale Production*, Productivity Press.

Peck, Martin (ed.) (2006) *Concrete: Design, Construction, Examples*, Birkhäuser.

Pfeifer, Gunter, Liebers, Antie M.and Brauneck, Per (2005) *Exposed Concrete*, Birkhäuser.

Pevsner Nikolaus (Second edn revised by Elizabeth Williamson) (1951) *The Buildings of England, Nottinghamshire*, Penguin (Yale University Press, 2000).

Raafat, Aly Ahmed (1958) *Reinforced Concrete In Architecture*, Reinhold Publishing Corp.

Rangan, B. V. and Warner, R. F. (1996) *Large Concrete Buildings*, Longman Group Ltd.

Román, Antonio (2002) *Eero Saarinen: An Architecture of Multiplicity*, Laurence King.

Rollo, Joe (2004) *Concrete Poetry: Concrete Architecture*, Cement Concrete and Aggregates Australia (CCAA).

Rollo, Joe (ed.) (2005) *Double Church near Freiburg, C+A*, Issue 01, Cement Concrete Aggregates Australia.

Rupasinghe, R. and Nolan, É. (2007) *Formwork for Modern, Efficient Concrete Construction*, BRE Press.

Sheil, Bob (ed.) (2005) *AD Special Edition: Design Through Making*, July/August.

Smith, Sean (2010) *How to Achieve Acoustic Performance in Masonry Homes*, Concrete Centre.

St John Wilson, Colin *et al.* (2006) *Sigurd Lewerentz*, Electa Architecture.

St John Wilson, Colin (2007) *The Other Tradition of Modern Architecture: The Uncompleted Project*, Black Dog Publishing.

Stirling, C. (2002) *Thermal Insulation: Avoiding Risks*, BRE Press.

Utzon, Jørn *et al.* (ed.) (2005) *Jørn Utzon Log Book Volume 11, Bagsvaerd Church*, Edition Bløndal.

Young, John (1978) *Designing with GRC: A Briefing Guide for Architects*, The Architectural Press Ltd.

Yvenes, M. and Madshus, E. (ed.) (2008) *Architect Sverre Fehn: Intuition, Reflection, Construction*, The National Museum of Art, Architecture and Design, Oslo.

Wurman, Richard S. (1986) *The Words of Louis I Kahn*, Rizzoli.

other sources of information

Building Research Establishment (2001) *Corrosion of Steel in Concrete - Protection and Remediation*, BRE Digest 444, BRE Press.

Building Maintenance Information (2001) *Life expectancy of Building Components. Surveyors' Experiences of Building in Use. A Practical Guide*, Building Cost Information Service Ltd.

CIRIA (1984) *Design of Shear Walls in Buildings*, CIRA Report 102, CIRIA.

Concrete Centre (2008) *Energy and CO_2: Achieving Targets with Concrete and Masonry*, Concrete Centre.

Concrete Industry (2009) *Sustainability Performance Report*, MPA.

Concrete Society (1986) *Concrete Detail Design*, Concrete Society with The Architectural Press.

CONSTRUCT (2010) *The National Structural Concrete Specification (NSCS)*, Concrete Structures Group.

selected websites

Canadian Plywood: www.canply.org

Concrete Centre: www.concretecentre.com

Concrete Quarterly Archive online (1947 to present): www.concretecentre.com

European Ready Mixed Concrete Organization: www.ermco.eu

US Green Building Council: www.usgbc.org

key standards and regulations

Building Regulations for England and Wales, Approved Documents Part A to P (see www.planningportal. gov.uk/england/professionals/buildingregs/ technicalguidance/bcapproveddocumentslist for the latest versions and detailed descriptions).

BS 6100-6.5:1987 *Glossary of building and civil engineering terms. Concrete and plaster. Formwork*

BS 6073-1: 1981 *Precast concrete masonry units. Specification for precast concrete masonry units*

BS 8007:1987 *The Code of Practice for the Design of Concrete Structures Retaining Aqueous Liquids*

BS 8500-1: 2006 *Concrete. Complementary British Standard to BS EN 206-1. Method of specifying and guidance for the specifier*

BS 8500-2: 2006

BS 8110-1:1997 *Structural use of concrete. Code of practice for design and construction*

BS EN 197-1: 2000 *Cement. Composition, specifications and conformity criteria for low heat common cements*

BS EN 933-7: 1998, *Tests for geometrical properties of aggregates. Determination of shell content. Percentage of shells in coarse aggregates*

BS EN 1097-6:2000, *Tests for mechanical and physical properties of aggregates. Determination of particle density and water absorption*

BS EN 1744-1: 2009 *Tests for chemical properties of aggregates. Chemical analysis*

BS EN 1991-1-1:2002 Eurocode 1: Actions on structures – Part 1-1: *General actions – Densities, self-weight and imposed loads*

[UK National Annex to Eurocode 1 Actions on structures – Part 1-1 : 2005,: *General actions – Densities, self-weight and imposed loads*]

BS EN 1992-1-1:2004 Eurocode 2: Design of Concrete Structures– Part 1-1: *General – Common rules for building and civil engineering structures*

BS EN 1992 -1-2:2004 Eurocode 2: *Structural Fire Design*

BS EN 12620: 2002 *Aggregates for Concrete*

BS EN 13263-1:2005+A1:2009 *Silica fume for concrete. Definitions, requirements and conformity criteria*

BS EN 15167-1: 2006 *Ground granulated blast furnace slag for use in concrete, mortar and grout. Definitions, specifications and conformity criteria*

European Union's Energy Performance of Buildings Directive (EPBD), see www.diag.org.uk

DIN V 18500:2006-12 *Cast stones - Terminology, requirements, testing, inspection*

ISO 140001: 2004, *Environmental Management Systems - Specification with guidance for use*

PD 6682-1:2003, *Aggregates. Aggregates for concrete. Guidance on the use of BS EN 12620*

index

image credits

Daici Ano, 4.56–4.58
Adams Kara Taylor, 1.14–1.18, 3.5
ARK-house arkkitehdit Oy, 4.61
Ove Arup & Partners, 1.4,1.5, 1.10,
   4.15, 8.12–8.15
Klaus Bang, 2.16
Sue Barr, 4.52, 4.53
BASF, 4.26–4.29
Bennetts Associates, 3.22, 3.23, 6.1,
   6.27, 9.8, 9.10–9.12, 10.20,
   10.21
Benson and Forsyth Architects, 9.27,
   9.29
Hervé Biele, 10.6–10.10
Hélèn Binet, 2.22, 4.62, 8.28, 9.26,
   10.13
Bison Concrete, p.143 (top)
Roger Bullivant, 5.8–5.10
Fekix Borkenau, 1.6
Tim Boyd, 1.2
Brookes Stacey Randall, 5.11
Brookes Stacey Randall and IAA
   Architecten, 3.16–3.18, 10.16
Caruso St John Architects, 4.63
Alan Chandler/Dirk Lellau 4.20–4.22
Peter Cook, 3.24, 10.1
Civil & Marine, 2.10
David Chipperfield Architects 8.34,
   8.35
Mario Cucinella Architects, 9.21–9.25
Williem Diepraam, 7.15
Thomas Dix, 9.2
drdh Architects, 4.34, 4.41
dRMM Architects, 5.1
Fawn Art Photography, 7.4

Ralph Feiner, 9.17
Guy Fehn, 1.8,1.9
Elizabeth Felicella, 2.1
Foster & Partners, 4.13,4.14, 4.11,
   p.141, 7.12
Eldridge Smerin, 4.37, 4.42, 4.43
Roger Gain, 2.6, 2.7
Chris Gascoingne, 3.1
Dennis Gilbert, 2.12
David Grandorge, 3.31
Rolande Hable, 3.13–15, 8.32, 8.33
Martine Hamilton Knight, 3.20, 6.19,
   10.18
Michael Has, 1.16
Herman Hertzberger, 7.13, 7.14, 7.16
Werner Huthmacher, 1.1
Keith Hunter, 9.9, 10.19
Alan Jones Architects, 4.44–4.47
Ben Johnson, 3.3
Klaus Kinold, frontispiece
Ian Lambot, 3.4
Nic Lehoux, 10.22, 10.24, 10.26,
   10.28
Thomas Leslie, 3.8
Jens Lindhe, 9.31
Thomas Mayer, 9.42, 9.43
Morphosis, 10.23, 10.25, 10.27
Adam Mørk, 9.30
Valerio Olgiati, 9.33–9.36
Peri, 4.6, 4.7 (drawings)
Piano and Rogers, 8.31
Remo Predreschi, 4.23
Price & Myers, 2.20
Richard Rogers and Partners, 7.8–7.10,
   8.29, 8.30

Christian Richters, 7.7, 9.39
RMJM, 2.13, 2.14, 4.48–4.50
Scala, 6.20
Paul Scott, 2.21
Frank J. Scherschel, 6.22
Hartwig Schneider 8.36, 8.37
Grant Smith, 4.1, 5.5, 6.18, 7.1
Sanaa, 9.44
Martin Spencer, 2.3, 3.6, 3.19,
   4.4–4.8, 4.11, 4.12, 4.36, 4.39,
   4.40, 4.60, 5.14, 6.7, 6.13–6.16,
   p.135, 8.6–8.9, 8.11, 9.7, 9.38,
   9.47, 9.48, 10.2
Margherita Spiluttini, 4.59, 9.5
Michael Stacey, 1.11, 1.12, 2.2 (left),
   3.27, 3.28, 3.33, 4.30–4.33, 4.35,
   4.51, 4.54, 6.6, 6.8, 6.17, 7.6,
   8.10, 8.17–8.21, 9.13,9.14, 9.19,
   9.20, 10.3–10.5
Michael Stacey Architects, 3.25. 3.32,
   5.7, 5.13
Tim Street-Porter, p.143 (bottom)
Schöck. 9.46, 9.49
Suffolk County Council, 3.10, 3.11,
   3.26, 3.29, 3.30
Edmund Sumner, Front cover, 9.1, 9.45
Tactility Factory, 4.24, 4.25
Trent Concrete, 3.21
View, 2.11,
Carl Wallace, 4.18
Ray Weitzenberg, 1.3
Gaston Wicky, 1.7
Nick Woods, 5.15
Stephen White, 1.13
Nigel Young, 9.37

Notes:
1. The drawings included in this guide, unless stated, have been
   prepared for this publication.
2. SI units have been used throughout this text.
3. The author and publisher have made every effort to contact
   copyright holders and will be happy to correct, in subsequent
   editions, any errors or omissions that are brought to their
   attention.